First Certificate
PASSKEY
Grammar Practice

DAVID McKEEGAN

MACMILLAN HEINEMANN
English Language Teaching

Published by Macmillan Heinemann ELT
Between Towns Road, Oxford, OX4 3PP
Macmillan Heinemann ELT is an imprint of
Macmillan Publishers Limited
Companies and representatives throughout the world

ISBN 0 435 24495 7 (with key)
    0 435 24496 5

Text © David McKeegan 1996
Design and illustration © Macmillan Publishers Limited 1998

Heinemann is a registered trademark of
Reed Educational & Professional Publishing Limited

First published 1996

The publishers would like to thank Michael Vince.

The author would like to thank his parents,
John and Ann McKeegan, and Kristi Larsen.

Printed in Thailand

2009 2008 2007 2006 2005 2004
17 16 15 14 13 12 11 10 9 8

Contents

Introduction

First Certificate PassKey Grammar Practice is designed to give students extra practice of the grammar points covered in PassKey, and to provide further examples of the type of tasks which appear in the Revised FCE Paper 3. Although the Passkey syllabus is followed quite closely, this workbook can be used to accompany any other coursebook at this level.

The new Paper 3 differs quite radically from the old one, so it is important that students are given the opportunity to become familiar with the format. For this reason most of the exercises in this book are based on Paper 3-type tasks.

Active control of grammar and vocabulary is what is tested in Paper 3, and each of the five task types focuses on these two areas with varying emphasis.

Part 1   Multiple-choice cloze
A cloze text with 15 gaps and 15 four-option multiple-choice questions. The emphasis is on vocabulary.

Part 2   Open cloze
A text with 15 gaps. The emphasis is on grammar.

Part 3   Key word transformations
10 separate items with a sentence which must be rewritten using a given key word. Most of the major FCE-level grammar structures are tested in this way, as well as vocabulary in the form of idioms and multi-word verbs.

Part 4   Error correction
A 15-line text containing errors. Some lines are correct, others contain an extra word. The emphasis is on grammar.

Part 5   Word formation
A text with 10 gaps. Each gap must be filled with the correct form of the word given at the end of each line. The emphasis is on vocabulary.

First impressions

1 Read the text and decide which answer A, B, C or D best fits each space.

Tattoos

Tattooing has been around for thousands of years. The **(0)** _B_ of making a permanent design or mark on the body was originally thought to **(1)** ___ magical protection against disease and misfortune. Later, it was used to show a person's **(2)** ___ status. The Romans, for example, **(3)** ___ to tattoo slaves and criminals.

With the **(4)** ___ of Christianity in Europe, tattooing was forbidden. It virtually **(5)** ___ out for hundreds of years, until European explorers came into **(6)** ___ with American Indians and Polynesians in the 17th and 18th centuries. Sailors would return from long **(7)** ___, decorated with large and elaborate designs. Many of these sailors later joined circuses, and **(8)** ___ a living by showing their tattoos to the public.

Nowadays, tattooing is **(9)** ___ as unusual, nor as popular as it once was. Tattoo parlours do **(10)** ___, but most people are unwilling to go **(11)** ___ the rather painful procedure. On the other hand, **(12)** ___ tattoos are becoming increasingly common. The design, which **(13)** ___ for three to six weeks, is painted painlessly onto the skin.

Other people still **(14)** ___ the original, permanent techniques, of course. The world record for the most-tattooed person is **(15)** ___ by Tom Leppard from Scotland. His leopard-skin design covers 99.2% of his body surface!

0	**A** effect	**B** act	**C** do	**D** fact
1	**A** prove	**B** do	**C** make	**D** provide
2	**A** senior	**B** society	**C** communal	**D** social
3	**A** used	**B** were	**C** could	**D** would
4	**A** coming	**B** arrival	**C** departure	**D** leaving
5	**A** died	**B** wore	**C** left	**D** went
6	**A** touch	**B** communication	**C** meeting	**D** contact
7	**A** travels	**B** sails	**C** voyages	**D** explorers
8	**A** paid	**B** worked	**C** did	**D** earned
9	**A** nowhere	**B** nor	**C** neither	**D** no
10	**A** be	**B** live	**C** exist	**D** stay
11	**A** through	**B** along	**C** under	**D** with
12	**A** short	**B** temporary	**C** part-time	**D** momentary
13	**A** lasts	**B** takes	**C** endures	**D** is
14	**A** rather	**B** wish	**C** elect	**D** prefer
15	**A** kept	**B** made	**C** held	**D** reached

The present simple and continuous

The present simple is used

● for permanent states

> *I **am** Scottish.* (I always will be)
> *I **work** in Geneva.* (I do now and I will do so for the foreseeable future)

● for habits and routines

> *She **cycles** to work every day.* (it's part of her daily routine)
> *She **cuts** her own hair.* (it's her habit to do so)

● for permanent truths and facts

> *The sun **rises** in the east and **sets** in the west.* (it's a fact of nature)

The present simple is often used with time adverbs such as:
usually, sometimes, never, every day , etc.

The present continuous is formed with: *to be* + present participle (*-ing* form)
It is used

● for actions happening at the moment of speaking

> *Look! The dog **is chasing** a rabbit.* (it is happening right now)

● for temporary situations

> *I'**m having** trouble finding a new job.* (not necessarily at this moment, but at this period in time which is –
> I hope – temporary)

The present continuous is often used with time adverbs like: *at the moment, now, today, at present*, etc.

---

2   Complete the sentences, putting the verbs in brackets into the present simple or continuous.

1 How much money *do you spend* (you/spend) on food every week?

2 Where is Ann?

   She _____ (sunbathe) in the garden.

3 _____ (you/watch) the TV?

   No. You can switch it off if you like.

4 I'm afraid I _____ (not/speak) Spanish very well.

5 John _____ (look) for a bigger flat.

6 She _____ (usually/finish) work before 6 o'clock.

7 _____ (you/know) how to use this computer program?

   Not yet. But I _____ (learn).

8 Where _____ (Joe/go) with that gun in his hand?

   Oh, he _____ (always/carry) it with him when he goes walking in the woods.

9 Be quiet! I _____ (think) Dad _____ (sleep) upstairs.

10 I _____ (not/like) cooking, but I _____ (love) eating.

3 Use the verbs below, in the present simple or continuous, to complete the sentences.

| wear | think | ~~speak~~ | do | make | have |

1 a Sally is very clever. She _speaks_ five languages.

   b I don't understand those people. What language _are they speaking_ ?

2 a He _____ a suit whenever he has an interview.

   b I _____ a raincoat because I think it might rain.

3 a I'm sorry, but I can't come out tonight. I _____ my homework.

   b My brother and I _____ the dishes after every meal.

4 a Do we have to go home now? We _____ such a good time!

   b She wants to go on holiday, but she doesn't think she _____ enough money.

5 a The car _____ an awful noise.

     Yes. Maybe we should stop at a garage.

   b How much money shall we invest in this project?

     Ask Mr Banks. He _____ the decisions in this company.

6 a What _____ of the new student?

     He seems very nice.

   b Jim looks very happy.

     He does, doesn't he? I wonder what he _____ about.

4 Underline the word or phrase which completes each sentence correctly.

1 She isn't having a birthday party _this year_/usually .

2 Why _are you crying_/do you cry? Have you hurt yourself?

3 The boss shouts _because/when_ he is angry.

4 You _work/are working_ for your father at the moment, aren't you?

5 I'm tidying my room _because Mum told/when Mum tells_ me to.

6 Do you listen to the radio _every day/, or can I turn it off_ ?

7 He goes to the opera _when he can afford it/to see 'Carmen'_ .

8 Something smells good! What _do you cook/are you cooking_?

9 I'm staying with my parents _temporarily/for two months every summer_ .

10 In autumn the leaves _fall/are falling_ from the trees.

5 Read the text below and look carefully at each line. If the line is correct put a tick (✓). If a line has a word which should not be there, write the word. There are two examples, (0) and (00).

Town and Country

0	The main advantage of living in a city is that there	✓
00	are so many things for to do in your free time. There	*for*
1	are cinemas, theatres, sports centres and stadiums. It	_____
2	is very much difficult to be bored in the city, as long as	_____
3	you have got money to spend. I do not think so I	_____
4	would like to living in the country because it is too	_____
5	quiet. People who are prefer the country say that it	_____
6	is much more relaxed than the city. They say that	_____
7	they do not worry about no crime, and that they enjoy	_____
8	breathing of clean air every day. I am sure that	_____
9	all this is true, but I think I would get bored out after	_____
10	only a few days. I do not like the traffic noise and	_____
11	air pollution of the city, but I can tolerate with it if it	_____
12	means I can spend all day making shopping, then go	_____
13	to the cinema and a night club in the evening. What is	_____
14	there to do in the country? Going for the long walks	_____
15	in the fields, surrounded about by trees and cows is	_____
	not my idea of a good time!	

Order of Adjectives

When using more than one adjective to describe a noun, there are some general rules to follow.

- 'Opinion' adjectives come before 'fact' adjectives in word order:

  *What a **beautiful silk** dress.* (It is my opinion that it is beautiful, but it is a fact that it is made of silk)

- Adjectives describing general qualities come before those describing particular qualities:

  *He drives a **big German** car.* (the car's size – 'big' – is a general quality, and the fact that it is German is more particular)

  Here is a general guide to the order of adjectives:

	opinion	*size/shape*	*colour*	*material/origin*	
A	**lovely**	**big**	**red**	**cotton**	jumper.

  It is, however, unusual to use more than three adjectives before a noun. One or two well-chosen adjectives are much more effective.

6 Put the adjectives in brackets into the correct position.

1 a big taxi (yellow) _a big yellow taxi_____.

2 a beautiful wooden desk (old) _____.

3 some blue flowers (plastic) _____.

4 a funny old film (American) _____.

5 a concrete building (huge) _____.

6 an expensive Italian racing car (red) _____.

7 a big leather sofa (comfortable) _____.

8 an ugly glass vase (pear-shaped) _____.

9 some little brown insects (horrible) _____.

10 a mysterious triangular object (metal) _____.

7 Fill in the gaps with the adjectives in the correct order.

1 She has green eyes. They are beautiful.

   She has _beautiful green_ eyes.

2 He rides a Japanese motorbike which is old and big.

   He rides a _____ _____ _____ motorbike.

3 She wore a beige raincoat. It was made of plastic.

   She wore a _____ _____ raincoat.

4 My shirt is long-sleeved, made of silk, and fashionable.

   I have a _____ _____ _____ shirt.

5 As a young man, he was pessimistic.

   He was a _____ _____ man.

8 Read the text below and think of the word which best fits each space. Use only one word in each space.

A Coincidence

A coincidence is an occasion **(0)** _when_ two or more things happen at the same time in an unusual or surprising way. Most people **(1)** _____ experienced coincidences. For example, a friend may telephone you **(2)** _____ the exact moment you were thinking about him. Coincidences happen all the **(3)**_____ , but few have been as remarkable **(4)** _____ the one experienced by King Umberto 1 of Italy.
On 28 July 1900, King Umberto went into a restaurant in Monza. He **(5)**_____ very surprised to find that the restaurant owner, **(6)** _____ was also called Umberto, looked and spoke exactly **(7)**_____ him. It was soon discovered that they were **(8)**_____ born in Turin on the same day. The restaurant owner had married a woman called Margherita, **(9)**_____ was also the name of the Queen whom King Umberto had married on the same day. What is more, the owner had opened his restaurant on the day **(10)** _____ the King's coronation.
The King was **(11)** _____ impressed that he invited the owner to an athletics meeting **(12)** _____ following day. Unfortunately, Umberto the restaurant owner died **(13)** _____ a mysterious shooting accident **(14)** _____ morning. Later that same day, King Umberto 1 was shot dead **(15)** _____ an anarchist.

In case

In case is a conjunction which means: because there might be (or might have been) a situation in which...

- When talking about the present or future, it is used with the present tense:

  *Lock the doors **in case** someone **tries** to break in.*

- When talking about the past, it is used with the past simple tense:

  *We took a bottle of water **in case** we **got** thirsty.*

- It is sometimes used with *should* when a present or future event is unlikely to happen:

  *The Prince of Wales and the Queen never travel together in the same plane **in case** it **should** crash.*

---

9 An explorer is going on an expedition into the jungle. Below is a list of things he is going to take, and the reasons for taking them. Match the objects with the reasons, and write sentences as in the example.

Object	Reason for taking
water	illness
rifle	friendly locals
medicine	thirst
map	help
presents	dangerous animals
mobile phone	getting lost

1 *He's taking some water in case he gets thirsty.* _____

2 *He's taking a rifle* _____ .

3 _____ .

4 _____ .

5 _____ .

6 _____ .

10 Complete the second sentence so that it has a similar meaning to the first sentence. Use the word in bold and other words. Use between two and five words.

1 You may need to contact me, so I'll give you my phone number.

   case

   I'll give you my phone number *in case you need* to contact me.

2 In case Tom comes home late we'll leave the door unlocked.

   because

   We'll leave the door unlocked _____ home late.

3 'Take a credit card, because you might run out of money,' he told us.

   case

   He told us to take a credit card _____ of money.

4 It is unlikely that you will need it, but take the tent with you anyway.

   should

   Take the tent with you _____ need it.

5   It is possible that no one will speak English, so you had better take this phrase-book with you.
   case
   You had better take this phrase-book with you _____ English.

6   In case you want a drink in the night, I'll leave some water by your bed.
   because
   I'll leave some water by your bed _____ a drink in the night.

7   The reason we took our camera was that we might have wanted to take some photos.
   case
   We took our camera _____ _____ to take some photos.

8   We may not see each other tomorrow, so I'll say goodbye now.
   case
   I'll say goodbye now _____ see each other tomorrow.

9   I'll give you my address in case you want to visit me in Scotland.
   might
   I'll give you my address _____ to visit me in Scotland.

10   There was a possibility that she might forget the number, so she wrote it on the back of her hand.
   case
   She wrote the number on the back of her hand _____ _____ it.

11   Use the word at the end of each line to form a word that fits in the space on the same line.

Nursing

Nursing is a job which demands great **(0)**___*strength*___	**STRONG**
of character. Most **(1)** _____ nurses work long	**PROFESSION**
hours and are underpaid. They make the **(2)** _____	**DECIDE**
to become nurses in the **(3)**_____ _____ that the job	**KNOW**
will never make them **(4)**_____ ; all they can hope	**WEALTH**
for is the **(5)**_____ that comes from helping	**SATISFY**
people who need them. **(6)** _____, nurses'	**UNFORTUNATE**
(7)_____ often seem to take advantage of this	**EMPLOY**
(8)_____ attitude, and make them work as many	**IDEAL**
hours as possible for very little money. So it is not	
(9)____ _____ that nurses sometimes become	**SURPRISE**
(10)_____ with their bosses, and decide to take	**PATIENT**
action to improve their working conditions.	

Work for a living

1 Read the text below and look carefully at each line. If the line is correct put a tick (✓). If a line has a word which should not be there, write the word. There are two examples (0) and (00).

Modelling

0	Many of young people dream about a career in modelling.	_of_
00	However, few of them realise exactly what it is like	✓
1	to be a professional model. It is not so all glamour and	_____
2	riches. For a start, only a few hopeful youngsters are	_____
3	actually make it as professionals. It can be very hurtful	_____
4	to be told that you do not have had what it takes. Those	_____
5	who do get regular work they are often surprised at	_____
6	how hard it can be. Getting up early in the morning	_____
7	and standing around for the hours in all kinds of	_____
8	weather is exhausting. The money may be quite as	_____
9	good, but it cannot go on forever. What do you do	_____
10	when you are too much old, and the model agency does	_____
11	not want you any more? Unless that you have made	_____
12	enough money to retire on by the time when you are	_____
13	thirty, then you might find yourself in financial	_____
14	trouble. To return up to the job market at that age,	_____
15	with no skills or experience to offer, could be a	_____
	nightmare.	

To be/get used to

● *To be used to* means 'to be accustomed to'.
It is used to talk about something that is normal for us in our everyday lives, and causes us no pain or difficulty.
It can be used with a noun or an *-ing* form.

> I **am used to getting up** at five in the morning. (I do it often and I find it easy)
> We **weren't used to** three meals a day. (It wasn't a normal part of our everyday lives)

● *To get used to* means 'to grow or become accustomed to'.
It is used to show how our feelings towards something change.
While *be used to* is about a state, *get used to* is about a process.
It is also used with a noun or *-ing* form.

> You **will get used to the traffic noise**, eventually. (In time, it will no longer bother you)
> He couldn't **get used to living** alone. (His feelings about living alone did not change - it was never pleasant for him)

2 Use the words below to complete the sentences with *(not) be/get used to* in the correct tense.

| spicy food | the noise | horses | obeying orders | ~~cycling~~ |
| the heat | flying | queuing | expensive restaurants | word processors |

1 Weren't you exhausted after such a long bicycle ride?

Not really. I *'m used to cycling.*

2 You can't just push in front of people at bus-stops, Mario! You'll have to _____.

3 Did you enjoy your Indian meal last night?

No, I didn't. I _____.

4 Brenda has used typewriters all her life. She is having trouble _____.

5 I am terrified of aeroplane journeys. I have never _____.

6 Living in such a hot climate was hard for the first year. But now we _____.

7 Since we moved to the city I haven't been able to sleep because of the traffic.

Don't worry. You'll _____.

8 Simon felt rather uncomfortable dining at the *Hilton* because he _____.

9 Did you find it difficult to adapt to life in the army?

Yes, I did. I _____.

10 When she started riding lessons she was quite nervous, but she is gradually _____.

3 Complete the second sentence so that it has a similar meaning to the first sentence. Use the word in bold and other words. Use between two and five words.

1 Being unfairly punished was beginning to feel normal to him.
   getting
   He _____ being unfairly punished.

2 Sleeping in a tent is an unusual experience for me.
   not
   I _____ in a tent.

3 Eventually, you will find it easy to milk the cow.
   used
   You _____ the cow eventually.

4 The neighbours' dog barking all night no longer bothers me.
   to
   I _____ the neighbours' dog barking all night now.

5 People can sometimes grow accustomed to loneliness.
   get
   People can sometimes _____ lonely.

6 Riding on the back of a motorcycle was a new experience for her.

to

She _____ on the back of a motorcycle.

7 I feel uncomfortable when there are animals in the house.

not

I _____ animals in the house.

8 Her new car no longer felt quite so strange to drive.

getting

She _____ her new car.

9 Gordon never became accustomed to life in prison.

used

Gordon never _____ a prisoner.

10 I often receive complaints from customers, so it is not a problem to me.

to

I _____ complaints from customers.

4 Read the text and decide which answer A, B, C or D best fits each space.

Margarine

Napoleon III of France was **(0)** _A_ for the invention of the butter substitute known as margarine. He was looking for a cheap **(1)** ___ to butter for the poorer people of society, and for his army and navy. So he **(2)** ___ up a prize competition to see who would **(3)** ___ up with the best solution.

There was only one **(4)** ___ into this competition, from a man called Mèges-Mouriès. He had **(5)** ___ over two years experimenting, and finally found an acceptable butter substitute made from milk and various animal fats. It tasted quite pleasant, and spread well on bread, but it was **(6)** ___ white. **(7)** ___ its colour, Mèges-Mouriès invention was awarded the prize. Yellow colouring was added to it at a **(8)** ___ date.

Margarine soon went into mass **(9)** ___ and was exported all over the world. In Britain it was called 'Butterine', until protests from farmers **(10)** ___ to that name being made illegal. Farmers in America were not happy **(11)** ___ the new arrival on the market either. They **(12)** ___ to the yellow colouring, saying that it made it resemble butter so **(13)** ___ that it could deceive consumers.

In effect, Napoleon III's competition is still going on. The ultimate **(14)** ___ of every margarine manufacturer is to produce a product that is **(15)** ___ to distinguish from butter. And they keep trying.

0	**A** responsible	**B** original	**C** fundamental	**D** vital
1	**A** option	**B** replacement	**C** alternative	**D** choice
2	**A** set	**B** took	**C** gave	**D** put
3	**A** make	**B** bring	**C** go	**D** come
4	**A** competitor	**B** player	**C** attempt	**D** entry
5	**A** used	**B** spent	**C** tried	**D** made
6	**A** clear	**B** pure	**C** true	**D** perfect
7	**A** Despite	**B** Although	**C** However	**D** Nevertheless

8	**A** further	**B** longer	**C** later	**D** farther
9	**A** production	**B** creation	**C** industry	**D** construction
10	**A** changed	**B** ended	**C** brought	**D** led
11	**A** over	**B** about	**C** at	**D** for
12	**A** protested	**B** objected	**C** disagreed	**D** argued
13	**A** justly	**B** nearly	**C** rightly	**D** closely
14	**A** end	**B** score	**C** goal	**D** finish
15	**A** impractical	**B** unable	**C** impossible	**D** incapable

The present perfect and past simple

The present perfect is formed with *have* + past participle.
It is used

- for actions which happened recently:

    I **have just seen** Paul. (It happened a few minutes ago)
    She **has spoken** to me recently. (In the not-too-distant past)

- for actions which have happened within a period up to and including the present:

    They **haven't been** to school this week. (It is still this week and they haven't gone to school during this period)
    He **has bought** a car. (Now he owns a car)

- for personal experiences or changes:

    He **has been** in prison. (It is one of his life experiences)
    She **has put on** a lot of weight. (It is a change which has happened to her)

The present perfect is often used with time adverbs like: *just, already, yet, since, so far, this week/month/year* etc.
The past simple is used for past habits, states or actions and does not have a connection with the present.

- It must be used if there is a reference to a past point in time.

    I **saw** that film **last week**.
    He **broke** his arm **when he was five**.

Compare these two sentences:
a *Ted and Sue went to New York for two weeks.*
b *Ted and Sue have gone to New York for two weeks.*
In sentence **a** Ted and Sue's trip to New York is over; but in sentence **b** they are still there.

5 Put the verbs in brackets into the present perfect or past simple.

1 *Have you heard* (you/hear) the latest news? A bomb *exploded* (explode) in the station at 10 o'clock this morning!

2 I can't find my diary. What _____ (you/do) with it?

   I _____ (put) it in your drawer last night.

3 I _____ (see) Steven when I was in Manchester. He _____ (not/change) at all.

4 She _____ (pass) her degree last year, then she _____ (get) a job in London.

5 Gary _____ (not/be) to work since he _____ (win) all that money.

6 I _____ (never/eat) octopus, but I _____ (eat) squid.

7 How many times _____ (you/be) to the cinema this year?

I _____ (go) twice in January, but I _____ (not/be) since then.

8 When _____ (Paul and Sue/get) married?

I don't know. I _____ (not/go) to their wedding.

9 Look at that! Someone _____ (leave) the fridge door open again!

It _____ (not/be) me. I _____ (not/be) in the kitchen for hours.

10 I _____ (just/read) your composition. It's very good. How much time _____ (you/spend) writing it?

11 We _____ (look) everywhere for a purple silk shirt, but we _____ (not/find) one yet.

_____ (you/try) Marks and Spencer yet? They _____ (have) one the last time I looked.

12 Tom! I _____ (not/see) you for ages!

Oh, hello Deborah! I'm sorry, I _____ (not/recognise) you at first. You _____ (lose) weight!

13 You _____ (work) very hard recently. I'm surprised the boss _____ (not/give) you a pay rise when you _____ (ask) him.

I'm not. That man _____ (never/like) me.

14 I _____ (learn) to speak a little Spanish when I was at school, but I _____ (never/have to) use it until the day I _____ (meet) Conchita. Since that day, I _____ (learn) a lot more.

15 Oh no! I think I _____ (break) Mum's stereo.

How _____ (you/do) that?

I _____ (try) to push a cassette into the CD player.

6 Underline the word or phrase which completes each sentence correctly.

1 Our team has won every game _this season_/last season.

2 _Did you lose/Have you lost_ your passport last summer?

3 Has Tracy met her boyfriend's parents _yet/yesterday_?

4 It _didn't snow/hasn't snowed_ very much last winter.

5 I have already told you _when you were thirteen/a thousand times_!

6 _Have you washed/Did you wash_ the car recently?

7 He did not meet any new people _since/in_ 1995.

8 People's lives have changed a lot _last/this_ century.

9 We _have never been/never went_ to Norway before.

10 I'm afraid I still _haven't heard/didn't hear_ from Eric.

7 Read the text below and think of the word which best fits each space. Use only one word in each space.

The Tungusaka Explosion

At 7.17 **(0)** _in_ the morning, on the 30th of June 1908, there was an enormous explosion in the Tungusaka region **(1)_____** Siberia. It destroyed around 40,000 trees in a circular area of about 15,400sq km. The force of the explosion **(2)_____** felt all over the world.

(3)_____ night in Siberia was known as the 'White Night'. It did not get dark because the sky was filled **(4)_____** bright silvery clouds. Even in London it was possible to read at midnight because the sky was **(5)_____** light. At the **(6)_____** time in other parts of Europe photographs could be **(7)_____** without the use of a flash.

How did it happen? Even today, nobody knows **(8)_____** sure. Some suggested that it was a UFO crash. Others thought that it was a meteorite. But when things fall to Earth **(9)_____** space they leave huge holes in the ground, called craters - and **(10)_____** was no crater in Tungusaka.

The **(11)_____** widely accepted explanation today **(12)_____** that it was a comet. A comet is a huge ball of dirty ice **(13)_____** flies through space, trailing a tail of dust behind it. If a piece of a comet broke off and entered the Earth's atmosphere, it would heat **(14)_____** and explode before it actually landed. The explosion would be huge, but it would **(15)_____** very little evidence of itself behind. Possibly just a cloud of silvery dust.

Comparatives

Regular adjectives follow these basic rules:
- one-syllable adjectives, and two syllable adjectives ending in -y form the comparison by adding -er.

  *young - young**er***
  *smart - smart**er***
  *dirty - dirt**ier***
  eg *I don't like you wearing make up. It makes you look **older**.*

- two-syllable adjectives ending in any other letter, three or more syllable adjectives, and adverbs ending in -ly form the comparison by adding *more*.

  *nervous - **more** nervous*
  *sensible - **more** sensible*
  *quickly - **more** quickly*
  eg *They say smoking relaxes you, but it really makes you **more nervous**.*

- Positive comparisons are made with *than*.
  *Rachel is **more intelligent than** Mark.*
  *He drives **more carefully than** you.*

- Equal comparisons are made with *as...as*.
  *Vicky is **as old as** Geoff.*
  *He sings **as beautifully as** an opera star.*

  or with *the same* +noun + *as*.

  *Vicky is **the same age as** Geoff.*

- Negative comparisons are made with *not as...as* or *less* + adj +*than*.
  *I'm **not as confident as** you or I'm **less confident than** you.*
  *She **does not behave as badly as** he does or She behaves **less badly than** he does.*

The most common irregular adjectives and adverbs are:
  good/well - better   bad/badly - worse   far - farther/ further

8 Complete the sentences using a comparative.

1 He has not got enough qualifications. We need someone who is _more qualified._

2 Your handwriting has not improved at all. In fact it has got _____.

3 Those boys are playing football too close to our house. I wish they would play _____ away.

4 I was surprised at how difficult it was to get a visa. I thought it would be _____.

5 Cheer up! Things are so bad at the moment that they can only get _____.

6 I thought the train would be cheaper than the plane, but I was surprised to find it was _____.

7 You are making a lot of careless mistakes. Try to work _____.

8 Scotland doesn't get much sunshine. I prefer to spend my holidays somewhere _____.

9 She gets annoyed if she has to wait for anything. She should try to be _____.

10 I still can't hear the television. Can you make it a bit _____?

9 Complete the second sentence so that it has a similar meaning to the first sentence. Use the word in bold and other words. Use between two and five words.

1 I will never weigh the same as my brother.
   be
   I will _____ as my brother.

2 The little boy said that his father was richer than my father.
   as
   'Your father is _____ my father,' said the little boy.

3 They say that dogs are not as intelligent as cats.
   more
   They say that cats _____ dogs.

4 She thinks Joyce is a better writer than Beckett.
   writes
   She does not think _____ Joyce.

5 My house and your house are equally expensive.
   as
   Your house _____ my house.

6 He does not travel as far as I do every week.
   than
   I travel _____ does every week.

7 This tree will soon be as tall as our house.
   same
   This tree will soon be _____ our house.

8 I speak French badly, but I think I speak it better than you.

than

I think you speak French _____ do.

9 My children behave better than your children.

as

Your children do not _____ my children.

10   They say men do not drive as safely as women.

drivers

They say women _____ men.

Multi-word verbs

10 Use the correct form of the multi-word verbs below to rewrite the second sentence so that it means exactly the same as the first sentence.

sort out	give up	go off	wear off	set up
grow up	wear out	get through	bring up	get on with

1 I don't think I'm going to **pass** the exams this year.

I don't think *I'm going to get through the exams this year.*

2 This milk tastes funny. I **don't think it's fresh any more**.

This milk tastes funny. I think _____.

3 Barry **resigned** from his job in order to go back to university.

Barry _____.

4 She has always dreamt of **starting** her own business.

She _____.

5 She **became less enthusiastic** about her job as time went on.

Her enthusiasm for her job _____.

6 Shaun has always **had a very good relationship with** his boss.

Shaun has always _____.

7 My parents **raised me** in France.

I was _____.

8 I need a new pair of boots. These ones have **grown so old that they are useless**.

I need a new pair of boots. These ones _____.

9 His mother is very good at **solving** other people's problems.

His mother _____.

10 **Stop behaving like a child!**

_____!

Out and about

The causative

The causative is formed with *to have* + object + past participle.
It is used when we cause someone else to do something for us, usually by paying them to do it.

I'm having my room redecorated. (I am paying a decorator to do it)

The tense is changed by altering the verb *to have*.

> She's **going to have a rose tattooed** on her arm.
> We **have had the carpets cleaned** recently.

Questions and negatives are formed with the auxiliary verb *do*.

> **Do you have your cat groomed** regularly?
> I **didn't have my tooth pulled out** after all.

The 'agent' (the person who does the job) is not usually included, unless it is particularly interesting or important.
> He had his central heating repaired **by the old lady next door**.

The verb *to get* is sometimes used in place of *to have*. This is slightly less formal.
> I finally **got my bike repaired** last week.

1 Complete the second sentence so that it has a similar meaning to the first sentence. Use the word in bold and other words. Use between two and five words.

1 I pay someone to wash my car every week.
   have
   I _have my car washed_ every week.

2 A builder is modernising our bungalow for us.
   having
   We _____ by a builder.

3 Does Giovanni design your clothes for you?
   designed
   Do _____ by Giovanni?

4 Nobody checked my homework last night.
   not
   I did _____ last night.

5 An accountant will have to check these books for you.
   get
   You will _____ these books checked by an accountant.

6 She has never made her own breakfast.

always

She has _____ for her.

7 I'm having my son taught chess by a grandmaster.

teaching

A grandmaster _____ chess.

8 The surgeon is not going to remove your appendix.

have

You are not going _____ removed.

9 Didn't you ask someone to translate this report yesterday?

get

Didn't you _____ yesterday?

10 My cat loves it when I scratch its head.

having

My cat _____ scratched.

2 Complete the sentences using the words in brackets.

1 We will _have the documents delivered_ (the documents/deliver) to you by motorcycle.

2 She couldn't understand the letter so she _____ (it/translate) by her German friend.

3 How often _____ (you/your eyes/test)?

4 Why _____ (you/this film/not develop) yesterday? Did you forget?

5 I will never _____ (my nose/pierce). I'm too frightened.

6 Our dog is very naughty. We should _____ (it/train) when it was a puppy.

7 They _____ (a new bathroom/fit) upstairs next week.

8 Look at Susan's hair! She must _____ (it/dye).

9 Your car is making a lot of noise. _____ (you/it/service) recently?

10 If we _____ (new computers/not install) soon, we will go out of business.

3 Use the word at the end of each line to form a word that fits in the space on the same line.

Home-workers

According to government research, more people are working
from home than ever before. **(0)** _Consequently_ , there has been   **CONSEQUENCE**
an increase in **(1)**_____ among those people who no longer   **LONELY**
have to travel to their place of **(2)**_____. Office workers   **EMPLOY**
spend their day **(3)**_____ by friends and colleagues, while   **SURROUND**
home-workers **(4)**_____ meet anyone face to face. The most   **RARE**
direct means of **(5)**_____ a home-worker has with the   **COMMUNICATE**
world **(6)**_____ is the telephone. The fax and the internet are   **OUT**

two more **(7)**_____ links that can be used, although they
still rely on the written, rather than the **(8)**_____, word.
What a home-worker really wants is the **(9)**_____ of
a human voice, not the **(10)**_____ bleeps of a computer.

TECHNOLOGY

SPEAK

WARM

DIGIT

The causative is also used to talk about accidents and misfortunes:

> I **had my wallet stolen** *yesterday*. (It was a misfortune that happened to me – I did **not** arrange for someone to steal my wallet!)
> He **got his leg broken** *in a karate match*. (It was an accident)

4 Rewrite the following sentences using the causative.

1 Someone burned down my brother's house.

My brother <u>had his house burned down</u>.

2 The police took away Darren's driving licence.

Darren _____.

3 His nose was broken in a car crash.

He _____.

4 All your money will be stolen if you go into that park at night.

You _____.

5 My face was scratched when I was playing with the cat.

I _____.

Needs + -ing

Needs +-ing is used when a certain job must be done, but we do not know – or care – who will do it:

> *This room* **needs tidying**. (It is a mess)
> *My stereo* **needs repairing**. (It is broken)

It is sometimes used as an indirect way of asking someone to do something:
> *The bathroom* **needs cleaning**. (= Clean the bathroom!)

5 Write sentences using *need* and one of the verbs below.

tidy   repair   service   feed   wash   cut   discipline

1 You hair looks very dirty. It *needs washing*.

2 The animals are hungry. They _____.

3 Your room is a mess. It _____.

4 These children have been very naughty. They _____.

5 Our TV is broken. It _____.

6 His hair is much too long. It _____.

7 My motorbike isn't running very well. It _____.

6 Read the text below and think of the word which best fits each space. Use only one word in each space.

The Dead Rabbit

You can imagine **(0)** _how_ upset Mr Bennet was when his pet Alsatian dog walked through the back door
(1) _____ a dead rabbit in its mouth. You can also imagine how anxious he became when he realised
(2) _____ the rabbit was, in fact, his next-door neighbours' pet, Fluffy. 'What **(3)** _____ we going to do?' he
said. 'They'll be furious when they **(4)** _____ out.'
Fortunately the rabbit had not **(5)** _____ badly damaged. The dog had just made it very dirty by playing
(6) _____ it. Poor Fluffy must **(7)** _____ died of fright. So Mr Bennet took it upstairs and **(8)** _____ it a good
wash and shampoo. He even blow-dried it. Then he took it outside and put it **(9)** _____ into its cage in the
neighbours' garden, hoping they **(10)** _____ think that it had died of natural causes.
The following day, Mr Bennet **(11)** _____ sitting in his garden, reading the paper, when the woman
(12) _____ next door appeared at the garden fence. She began to **(13)** _____ him how upset her little girl
was. 'What happened?' asked Mr Bennet, trying **(14)** _____ look innocent.
'Poor Fluffy died **(15)** _____ Wednesday, and we buried it,' she explained. 'But this morning it was back in its
cage!'

Genitive -'s and -s'

The genitive is used to show possession. It is always placed before the noun that is possessed.

> The **dog's** bone.

To form the genitive place -'s after any singular noun, or -' after a noun in the plural ending in -s.

> A **lady's** car. (one lady)
> The two **boys'** father. (two boys)

After an irregular plural form -'s is added.

> The **people's** palace.
> The **women's** changing-room

When something belongs to two or more people, -'s is placed after the last name mentioned.

> **Dave** and **Trudy's** swimming pool.

---

7 Rewrite these sentences using a genitive form.

1 This car belongs to my friend. This is _my friend's car._

2 The bag belonged to someone else. It was _____.

3 Terry and Judy will soon own that farm. That will soon be _____.

4 Is anybody sitting in this seat? Is this _____?

5 Don't get involved in the problems of other people. Don't get involved _____.

6 Those toys do not belong to you. They _____.

7 Did you go to the wedding of John and Paula? Did you go _____?

8 My parents own this building. This is _____.

8 Read the text below and look carefully at each line. If the line is correct put a tick (✔). If a line has a word which should not be there, write the word. There are two examples (0) and (00).

My hobby

0	I started to learning the guitar when I was ten years old.	*to*
00	I am seventeen now, so I have been playing for seven	✓
1	years since. My first guitar was a present from my uncle.	_____
2	It was very old and needed for repairing, but I loved it and	_____
3	used to play it until my fingers they hurt. On my twelfth	_____
4	birthday, my father bought me a brand-new one, and I	_____
5	started going to private guitar lessons. My teacher she	_____
6	teaches classical guitar, which I much like, but I really	_____
7	want to play the rock music. Sometimes I play an electric	_____
8	guitar. It is very loud and my mother hates it. Unfortunately	_____
9	it is not mine, it is of my friend's.	_____
10	My ambition is to play in a rock band and make records. I	_____
11	would like for to travel around the world, playing in different	_____
12	countries. My friend is a good singer, so we are going to be	_____
13	form a band together. All we need to do is find out a	_____
14	drummer and a bass player. I will write some songs and	_____
15	we will practise in my bedroom. I'm sure about my mother won't mind.	_____

For and *since*

For and *since* are usually used with a perfect tense.

- *For* is used before a length of time. It answers the question 'How long?' (*For* is frequently used with the past simple in this way.)
  *I haven't seen her **for five years.***
  *She had been working there **for two weeks.***

- *Since* is used before a point in time. It answers the question 'From what time?'
  *He has lived here **since he was a boy**.*
  *I've been feeling ill **since my birthday.***

BUT *Since* can be used with a length of time and the past simple in this construction: *It is..* + length of time + *since* + past simple:
  ***It's years since** I **saw** Jim.*
  ***It's two weeks since** she **phoned** me.*

9 Underline the word or phrase which completes each sentence correctly.

1 I haven't had my eyes examined <u>for</u>/since years.

2 She has lived in this flat since *twenty years/she was a little girl.*

3 It's two months since my sister *wrote/has written* to me.

4 We haven't been to the cinema since *ages/they closed it down.*

5 Have you been waiting *for/since* a long time?

6   It's *January/months* since I went out for a meal.

7   The bread has been in the oven *for/since* long enough now.

8   I've been trying to contact Brian since *all day/this morning*.

9   By 1998, I will have lived in this town *since 1993/for five years*.

10   I've owned this bicycle *for/since* as long as I can remember.

10 Complete the second sentence so that it has a similar meaning to the first sentence. Use the word in bold and other words. Use between two and five words.

1   I started working here 30 years ago, and I'm still working here.
    here
    I *have been working here for* 30 years.

2   She hasn't spoken to her brother-in-law for ages.
    spoke
    It's _____ to her brother-in-law.

3   The last time I had my car serviced was February.
    since
    I haven't _____ February.

4   The baby started crying at 8 o'clock this morning, and it still hasn't stopped.
    been
    The baby _____ 8 o'clock this morning.

5   Five years have passed since our wedding day.
    married
    We _____ _____ five years.

6   It has been a long time since I went sailing.
    not
    I _____ a long time.

7   We moved to this city sixteen years ago.
    in
    We have been _____ sixteen years.

8   When they opened the new sports centre I started training every day.
    been
    I have _____ they opened the new sports centre.

9   The last time Sally saw her parents was 1994.
    seen
    Sally has _____ 1994.

10   You haven't bought me a meal for ages.
    since
    It's _____ me a meal.

11 Read the text and decide which answer A, B, C or D best fits each space.

Street papers

The **(0)** _B_ of homelessness is an international one. In the capital cities of the world, the **(1)** ____ of people begging on the streets is becoming increasingly **(2)** ____ . But all over the world, homeless people are taking the future into their own **(3)** ____ . By selling 'street papers' they no longer need to beg for a **(4)** ____.

The concept of the street paper is **(5)** ____. It is sold by homeless and ex-homeless people who buy it at a **(6)** ____ price of 30p and sell it to the public for 70p, keeping 40p for themselves. If they have no money, then they can get the first ten copies on **(7)** ____ and pay for them later. Every paper seller receives training and is given a special **(8)** ____ badge.

The paper itself **(9)** ____ articles of general and social interest, film and book **(10)** ____, cartoons and the **(11)** ____ celebrity interview. Advertising and sales **(12)** ____ most of the income, and all profits go **(13)** ____ into helping homeless people.

The Big Issue is the street paper of the British homeless. It was set up in 1991, and **(14)** ____ then it has helped hundreds of people to get **(15)** ____ the streets and back into society.

0	**A** trouble	**B** problem	**C** difficulty	**D** chaos
1	**A** sight	**B** vision	**C** look	**D** view
2	**A** usual	**B** common	**C** rare	**D** routine
3	**A** heads	**B** shoulders	**C** hands	**D** mouths
4	**A** life	**B** living	**C** being	**D** pay
5	**A** easy	**B** straight	**C** plain	**D** simple
6	**A** stuck	**B** steady	**C** held	**D** fixed
7	**A** credit	**B** cheque	**C** cash	**D** card
8	**A** character	**B** personality	**C** manner	**D** identity
9	**A** consists	**B** contains	**C** keeps	**D** involves
10	**A** stories	**B** reviews	**C** opinions	**D** views
11	**A** sometimes	**B** often	**C** occasional	**D** seldom
12	**A** give	**B** provide	**C** show	**D** offer
13	**A** back	**B** out	**C** through	**D** forward
14	**A** from	**B** of	**C** for	**D** since
15	**A** out	**B** away	**C** off	**D** up

Crime wave

1 Read the text below and look carefully at each line. If the line is correct put a tick (✔). If a line has a word which should not be there, write the word. There are two examples, (0) and (00).

The worst day

0	One of the most worst days of my life was when we	_most_
00	returned from holiday one summer to find that	✓
1	our house had been burgled. The place it was a	_____
2	mess. The burglars had been stolen the TV, the video	_____
3	recorder, the stereo and all lot of our records and CDs.	_____
4	All the drawers had been emptied and their contents	_____
5	thrown around the room. We phoned out the police, who	_____
6	sent two their officers around very quickly. They looked	_____
7	at the mess, and asked about a few questions. I asked	_____
8	them if they were going to check for fingerprints, but they	_____
9	said there was no point. They told to us that it was very	_____
10	unlikely that the burglars would be caught anyway.	_____
11	We all felt very angry and confused. At the least we	_____
12	were insured, which had meant that we were able to	_____
13	replace nearly everything of that had been stolen. But we	_____
14	couldn't replace the feeling of security that we had	_____
15	before the burglary happened us. Even today, one year	_____
	later, we still worry that it may happen again.	_____

The past continuous and the past simple

The past continuous is formed with: the past of *to be* + present participle.
It is used to talk about events which began in the past, but still had not finished at a specific time in the past:

> I **was washing** *my hair at seven o'clock last night.* (I started washing it before seven o'clock, and I still hadn't finished when the clock struck seven.)

The past simple is used

- to talk about events which happened one after the other:

> She **ran out** *of the house,* **jumped** *on her bike, and* **rode** *off.*

- to talk about completed actions in the past:

> He **wrote** *a novel last year.*

The past continuous and past simple are used together when

- a continuous past action is interrupted by another past action:

  We **were playing** in the garden when it **started** to rain.

- a past action takes place during another, longer past action or state:

  He **met** his wife while he **was living** in Portugal.
  While I **was working** for the Health Service I **decided** to give up smoking.

---

2   Put the verbs in brackets into the past simple or continuous.

1 I _was watching_ (watch) TV when Mark _phoned_ (phone).

2 What _____ (you/do) at the time of the murder?

3 She _____ (jump) into the river and _____ (rescue) the drowning boy.

4 I _____ (see) my first baseball game while I _____ (live) in New York.

5 Where _____ (you/go) when you _____ (get off) the train?

6 We _____ (ring) the police because the neighbours _____ (play) their music too loud.

7 He _____ (write) the whole composition during the lunch hour.

8 She _____ (write) to her brother when he _____ (walk) through the front door.

9 _____ (you/work) in Spain this time last year?

   Yes. I _____ (go) out there in '93.

10 Mum and Dad _____ (sleep) when I _____ (get) home last night.

11 What _____ (that news reader/say) just then?

    I don't know. I _____ (not/listen).

12 Someone _____ (take) a photo of me while I _____ (have) a bath.

13 _____ (you/see) the match last night?

    No. I _____ (try) to get some work done.

14 We _____ (not/know) what to do when the computer _____ (break down).

15 It _____ (rain) outside and the children _____ (cry), so we _____ (decide) to play a game.

3   Correct the sentences which are wrong, and put a tick (✓) by the ones which are correct.

1 The kitchen caught fire while we were having dinner.

   ✓ _____.

2 The sun shone so we decided to go for a walk.

   The sun was shining so we decided to go for a walk. _____

3 I'm afraid I wasn't hearing what you said.

   _ _____.

4 Alan read a newspaper when he heard a strange noise.

   _ _____.

5 She was knowing she was being followed.

    _ _____.

6 The boss walked in while I played a computer game.

    _ _____.

7 I was walking home from work when a dog attacked me.

    _ _____.

8 He was reading the entire book, from start to finish, in two hours.

    _ _____.

9 What did you do when you saw someone trying to steal your car?

    _ _____.

10 I didn't see the last goal because I looked at the sky at the time.

    _ _____.

Making deductions

- When talking about possibilities in the past we use *may/might/could* + *have* + past participle:

    *She **may have lost** your phone number.* (It is possible that that is the reason she has not phoned you.)
    *It **could have been** Tom who broke the radio.* (It is possible that it was Tom.)

    Only *may* and *might* are used in the negative when talking about possibilities:

    *They **may/might not have heard** you correctly.* (It is possible that they thought you said something else.)

Note: *They **couldn't have heard** you correctly.* = It is certain that they thought you said something else.

- When making logical deductions about the past we use *must/can't* + *have* + past participle:

    *Robert **must have lied** to me.* (There is no other possibility. It is certain.)
    *He **can't have told** the police.* (It is impossible.)

4 Complete the second sentence so that it has a similar meaning to the first sentence. Use the word in bold and other words. Use between two and five words.

1 It is possible that you gave her the wrong number.
    might
    You _____ the wrong number.

2 It is not possible that Richard knew about this.
    have
    Richard _____ about this.

3 Perhaps Susan didn't want to come to the party.
    may
    Susan _____ to come to the party.

4 There is a possibility that Mary forgot about the meeting.
    could
    Mary _____ about the meeting.

5 I am certain that he was not telling the truth.

must

He _____ lies.

6 He might have seen the film already.

has

Perhaps _____ the film.

7 The police say his death was definitely not an accident.

been

The police say his death _____ an accident.

8 There is no doubt that he was driving too fast at the time.

must

He _____ too fast at the time.

9 Perhaps Colin was in the bath when you phoned.

might

Colin _____ in the bath when you phoned.

10 It is possible that she did not receive my letter.

may

She _____ my letter.

5 Underline the word or phrase that completes each sentence correctly.

1 I'm not certain, but it *might*/*must* have been half past four.

2 You *must*/*can't* have been sunbathing all week - you haven't got a tan.

3 Why don't you sit down? You *may*/*must* be exhausted after such a long journey.

4 He was foolish to chase the robber. He *can't*/*could* have been killed.

5 She *can't*/*must* have gone on holiday. She's got too much work to do.

6 It *can't*/*must* have been Tom who left the lights on. He's always doing that.

7 Laura *may*/*can't* have tried to phone earlier, but I don't know for sure.

8 He *must*/*might* have picked up this gun because his fingerprints are all over it.

9 She *can't*/*could* have eaten that whole cake herself - it was huge!

10 Simon *must*/*may* have been mad to do something like that.

6 Read the text below and think of the word which best fits each space. Use only one word in each space.

Beethoven

Ludwig van Beethoven, **(0)** <u>one</u> of the most popular classical composers of all time, **(1)** _____ sometimes known as 'the Shakespeare of music'. He was born in Bonn in 1770, **(2)** _____ published his first work **(3)** _____ the age of thirteen. Mozart was his teacher **(4)** _____ a short time, although they did not **(5)** _____ on very well together; Beethoven was a difficult student.

As a composer, Beethoven was a genius – but as a person, he was not very easy **(6)** _____ like. He was a passionate man **(7)** _____ lost his temper very easily. He was also arrogant. The upper classes of Vienna used to **(8)** _____ him to parties, where he was often quite rude. He was once heard to say to a prince: 'There **(9)** _____ always be many princes, but there is only **(10)** _____ Beethoven'. Nevertheless, Beethoven composed some of the most beautiful symphonies the world **(11)** _____ ever heard. How was **(12)** _____ an arrogant, bad-tempered man inspired to write such romantic music? Perhaps the answer lies in the three letters **(13)** _____ were found after his death. They were addressed to his 'Immortal Beloved'. **(14)** _____ knows who this woman was, but it appears that Beethoven was deeply in love **(15)** _____ her for most of his adult life.

Relative pronouns and adverbs

The relative pronouns used for people are:

- *who/that* (subject)
  *An opportunist is a person **who/that** takes every chance they get.*

- *whom* (object)
  *Is that the woman **whom** (or: **who/that**) they arrested?*

- *whose* (possessive)
  *A widow is a woman **whose** husband is dead.*

The relative pronouns used for things and animals are:

- *which/that* (subject or object)
  *There's the dog **which/that** bit me!*
  *Where is the car **which/that** you stole?*

- *whose/of which*
  *That is the chair **whose leg/the leg of which** is broken.*

The relative adverbs are:

- *where* (in, on, at, to which place)
  *This is the town **where** I was born.*

- *when* (in, on, at which time)
  *1945 was the year **when** the war ended.*

- *why* (for, because of which)
  *This is the reason **why** I'm so happy.*

When a relative pronoun or adverb is the object of the verb in the relative clause, it can be omitted.
  Is that the woman they arrested?
  Where is the car you stole?
  1945 was the year the war ended.
  This is the reason I'm so happy.

7 Fill in the gaps with an appropriate relative pronoun or adverb, **where necessary**.

1 A carpenter is a person <u>who </u>works with wood.

2 The Isle of Man is the island _____ the Tourist Trophy races are held.

3 There is the woman _____ daughter is an actress.

4 1964 was the year _____ my mother graduated from university.

5 There may soon come a time _____ all work is done by machines.

6 Can you tell me the reason _____ I have to do all this work?

7 I want you to buy the TV _____ has the largest screen.

8 Is that the old man _____ had his TV stolen yesterday?

9 7am was the time _____ we all had to get out of bed.

10 We spent a night in a house _____ was supposed to be haunted.

8 Complete the second sentence so that it has a similar meaning to the first sentence. Use the word in bold and other words. Use between two and five words.

1 A friend of mine owns four Mercedes.
   who
   I have _____ four Mercedes.

2 We had this room redecorated last year.
   which
   This _____ we had redecorated last year.

3 My cat just sleeps in front of the fire all day.
   that
   I have _____ in front of the fire all day.

4 He is very fit because he trains every day.
   why
   The _____ so fit is because he trains every day.

5 Queen Victoria was born in 1819.
   when
   1819 _____ Queen Victoria was born.

6 I borrowed a calculator from that girl.
   whose
   That is _____ I borrowed.

7 Did they interview this man last night?
   whom
   Is this _____ last night?

8 Both of her brothers are in the Navy.
   who
   She has _____ in the Navy.

9 He has a house whose roof needs repairing.
   which
   He has a house _____ needs repairing.

10 My father was brought up in this town.
   where
   This is _____ my father was brought up.

9 Read the text and decide which answer A, B, C or D best fits each space.

The *Mary Celeste*

The *Mary Celeste* had always been **(0)** _B_ an unlucky ship, but no one could have predicted what would happen to it when it **(1)** _____ sail from New York in November 1872. It was **(2)** _____ for Genoa with a cargo of alcohol - a **(3)** _____ which should have taken about five weeks. However, Captain Briggs, his wife, his two-year-old daughter, and the crew of seven sailors were never seen **(4)** _____ .

The *Mary Celeste* was **(5)**_____ off the Azores by a British ship called the *Dei Gratia*. It appeared to be in trouble, so Captain Morehouse sailed closer in order to **(6)** _____ . Nobody answered his calls, so he sent three sailors in a boat to **(7)** _____ help. They **(8)** _____ the ship totally deserted.

Some of the sails had been slightly **(9)**_____ by a storm but, **(10)** _____ from that, the *Mary Celeste* was in perfect **(11)** _____ . One small boat was missing, along with a map, and some navigation equipment. So it was **(12)** _____ that the crew had left the ship voluntarily. But why would they have left a large, safe ship in good **(13)** _____ order for a much smaller, weaker boat?

Many **(14)** _____ have been made to explain this mystery. Could it have been pirates? Nothing was stolen. An attack by a sea monster? The ship was not damaged. UFOs? Ghosts? To this day, no one has offered an explanation which is entirely **(15)** _____ .

0	**A** believed	**B** considered	**C** known	**D** regarded
1	**A** made	**B** set	**C** gave	**D** went
2	**A** heading	**B** travelling	**C** running	**D** going
3	**A** travel	**B** sail	**C** cruise	**D** journey
4	**A** later	**B** once	**C** more	**D** again
5	**A** looked	**B** spotted	**C** noted	**D** watched
6	**A** detect	**B** test	**C** experiment	**D** investigate
7	**A** put	**B** offer	**C** hand	**D** serve
8	**A** searched	**B** found	**C** saw	**D** met
9	**A** hurt	**B** injured	**C** damaged	**D** broken
10	**A** except	**B** apart	**C** far	**D** away
11	**A** condition	**B** state	**C** way	**D** health
12	**A** clean	**B** actual	**C** clear	**D** transparent
13	**A** going	**B** operating	**C** standing	**D** working
14	**A** tries	**B** goes	**C** turns	**D** attempts
15	**A** complete	**B** satisfactory	**C** enough	**D** efficient

Multi-word verbs

10 Use the correct form of the multi-word verbs below to rewrite the second sentence so that it means exactly the same as the first sentence.

put off	call off	settle up	get away with	take up
carry out	pick up	go through	drop out	work out

1 £5,000 in cash was the amount of money the robbers **succeeded in stealing**.

The robbers _got away with £5,000 in cash_.

2 Why did you decide **to cancel** the match?

Why _____?

3 He **is collected** from school every day by his mother.

Every day his mother _____.

4 This problem is going to take some time **to solve**.

It is going to take _____.

5 She **spends** a lot of her time looking after sick animals.

Looking after sick animals _____.

6 I got my Dad **to examine** my homework before I handed it in.

My Dad _____.

7 Do you know who **was responsible for** this terrible crime?

Do you know _____?

8 He **didn't complete** the course because he found a job in marketing.

He _____.

9 **I was discouraged from** entering the building because there was a large dog in the doorway.

The large dog in the doorway_____.

10 You don't have to pay now. You can **pay in full** at the end of the month.

You don't have to pay now. You _____.

Playing the game

1   Read the text below and think of the word which best fits each space. Use only one word in each space.

A Mistake

One Christmas eve, the Stopes family **(0)** <u>were</u> invited to stay at their friends' new house in Scotland. As it was very **(1)**_____ away, and the Stopes would not be **(2)**_____ to arrive before midnight, their friends agreed **(3)**_____ leave the gate open and put the key under a rock outside the front door. In **(4)**_____ way, the Stopes could let themselves in **(5)**_____ waking their friends up.

The map that their friends **(6)**_____ drawn for them was not very good, so they did not find the house **(7)**_____ about 1 o'clock in the morning. The gate **(8)**_____ locked so Gary, the eldest of the three brothers, climbed over and unlocked **(9)**_____ from the inside. The family marched towards the house and began to look **(10)**_____ the front door key. Before they found it, however, the father whispered that the back door had **(11)**_____ left open anyway, so they all got in through that.

It had been a long tiring journey, so the Stopes **(12)**_____ themselves some tea and sandwiches. All the time they kept very quiet so **(13)**_____ not to wake up their friends. At one thirty in the morning they crept upstairs and found three empty rooms **(14)**_____ which to sleep. The **(15)**_____ morning, Christmas day, they came downstairs and found two complete strangers sitting at the table. The whole family had accidentally broken into the house next door!

Used to

Used to describes a past habit or state.

> I **used to** go jogging every morning. (past habit)
> She **used to** live in Germany. (past state)

Negatives and questions are normally formed with the auxiliary *do*, and *used* changes to *use*.

> No, he **didn't use to** work for me.
> **Did you use to** play hockey at school?

Would can replace *used to* only when it describes a past habit.

> We **would/used to** watch baseball every Sunday.

> BUT: I **used to** have a toboggan. (NOT *would have* because *have* is used here for possession.)

To talk about present habits, use *usually*.

> I **usually** train three times a week.

2 Complete the second sentence so that it has a similar meaning to the first sentence. Use the word in bold and other words. Use between two and five words.

1 Her father took her to the dentist twice a year when she was a child.
to
When she was a child, her father _____ to the dentist twice a year.

2 When I was at university, I used to go to the library every day.
would
When I was at university, _____ to the library every day.

3 Spending all day in bed is not something I would normally do.
usually
I _____ all day in bed.

4 He used to listen to listen to rock music when he was a teenager - not disco music.
did
He _____ to disco music when he was a teenager - he used to listen to rock music.

5 Crashing his bike was something that Barry did quite regularly.
to
Barry _____ quite regularly.

6 It is not my habit to lend money to people, but you can borrow £10 if you want.
usually
I _____ to people, but you can borrow £10 if you want.

7 My brother and I used to play badminton in the park every Saturday.
would
Every Saturday, my brother and I _____ in the park.

8 Were you a regular visitor to the health club in Edinburgh?
to
Did _____ the health club in Edinburgh regularly?

9 Going out to restaurants was not something we did very often.
use
We _____ out to restaurants very often.

10 They never used to take a map with them when they went on mountain walks.
would
They _____ with them when they went on mountain walks.

3 Fill in the gaps with *usually, use(d) to* or *would* and a suitable verb.

1 I went to school by bus this morning, but I *usually go* by car.

2 Wendy has given up coffee. She _____ ten cups a day.

3 I really like cabbage now, but when I was a child I _____ it.

4 It surprises me that Fred does so much sport nowadays. When we were at school he _____ hate it.

5 I'm sure I've seen you somewhere before. _____ in Newcastle?

6 It is not like Gordon to be late for work. He _____ very punctual.

7 When we were students _____ to the theatre about twice a month.

8 That supermarket has been built recently. There _____ a cinema there, didn't there?

9 Anna and I often have long conversations these days. This is nice, because we _____ to each other at all.

10 Steven looks unusually smart today. He _____ a tie, does he?

4 Use the word at the end of each line to form a word that fits in the space on the same line.

Mountaineering

Mountaineering is an almost unique sport, as the **(0)** _climber_	**CLIMB**
is in **(1)**_____ with nature itself rather than with other	**COMPETE**
humans. For this reason it is an extremely **(2)**_____	**DANGER**
activity. Nature does not follow any rules or **(3)**_____,	**REGULATE**
and can often play very **(4)**_____.	**FAIR**
(5)_____ mountaineers are quite aware of the risks	**PROFESSION**
involved in their sport. Although they are **(6)**_____	**ADVENTURE**
spirits at heart, they have a full **(7)**_____ of the	**UNDERSTAND**
vital **(8)**_____ measures necessary to keep them alive, and	**SAFE**
never **(9)**_____ put themselves in needless danger. On	**KNOW**
the other hand, they say that the sense of **(10)** _____ at	**ACHIEVE**
the end of a climb is directly proportional to the risks involved.	

Past perfect

The past perfect is formed with _had_ + past participle.
In many ways it is simply the past equivalent of the present perfect.

> I **had just seen** Mary. (not long before a specific time in the past)
> They **hadn't been** to school that week. (for a period of time up to and including a specific time in the past)
> He **had been** in prison. (it was one of his life experiences)

It is used in narratives to indicate which event happened first.
Compare these two sentences:

a _When we arrived at the stadium, the match **started**._
b _When we arrived at the stadium, the match **had started**._

In sentence **a** they saw the whole game, from start to finish; but in sentence **b** they missed the kick-off.

5 Put the verbs in brackets into the past simple or past perfect.

1 When we returned to the car we _saw_ (saw) that someone _had smashed_ (smash) the windows.

2 I _____ (realise) I _____ (lose) my purse when I opened my bag.

3 He _____ (lose) the squash game because he _____ (never/play) squash before in his life.

4 David _____ (buy) his ticket the week before, so I don't understand why he _____ (try) to get in without paying.

5 By the time she _____ (be) eighteen she _____ (visit) nearly every capital city in the world.

6 Paula _____ (drop) the cup she was holding and _____ (burst) into tears.

7 Why _____ (you/not/speak) to Jim at the meeting yesterday?

Because he _____ (leave) by the time I got there.

8 Sally was upset when _____ (you/not/eat) any of her birthday cake.

I _____ (not/can) help it. I _____ (just/eat) a huge meal.

9 You _____ (look) happy when you were talking to Jackie last night.

Yes. I _____ (not/see) her for six years.

10 It _____ (take) nearly four hours to drive to the garden party, and when we _____ (get) there they _____ (refuse) to let us in!

Why?

Because we _____ (forget) to bring our invitations.

11 Johnny _____ (spent) seven years of his life in prison before he _____ (realise) that the things he _____ (done) to get there were wrong. He _____ (rob) banks, he _____ (burgle) houses, he _____ (steal) cars. But, fortunately, he _____ (never/kill) anyone.

6 Complete the second sentence so that it has a similar meaning to the first sentence. Use the word in bold and other words. Use between two and five words.

1 Barry was very excited because it was his first time on television.

never

Barry _____ before, so he was very excited.

2 The children ran over the bridge to see the fire engine, but it was no longer there.

had

The fire engine _____ time the children ran over the bridge.

3 He looked familiar to me, but in fact he was a complete stranger.

met

Although he looked familiar to me, I _____ before.

4 After they had had the contract read by a lawyer, they signed it.

before

They had the contract read by a lawyer _____ it.

5 Staying in a five-star hotel was a new experience for us.

stayed

We _____ in a five-star hotel before.

6 They arrived at the cinema just in time to see 'The End' come up on the screen.
   just
   The film _____ by the time they arrived at the cinema.

7 He had to write over fifty letters to get an interview.
   had
   He got an interview only after _____ over fifty letters.

8 She left the office after turning off all the lights.
   turned
   After _____ all the lights, she left the office.

9 When we arrived at the house, Dan had just left.
   soon
   Dan left the house and _____ after.

10 I checked that I had my passport with me before I left for the airport.
   after
   I left for the airport _____ that I had my passport with me.

7 Read the text and decide which answer A, B, C or D best fits each space.

Déjà vu

Have you ever been in a **(0)** _B_ in which you suddenly thought 'I've been here before'? That strange **(1)** _____ of having had exactly the same experience at some unknown time in the past is **(2)** _____ as *déjà vu*. Most people have had this feeling at one time or **(3)** _____, but no one has come up with a satisfactory **(4)** _____ of what *déjà vu* actually is.

There are the usual eccentric theories **(5)** _____ memories of a previous life, or of some **(6)** _____ - forgotten 'out-of-body experience'. Others **(7)** ____ that a *déjà vu* is the memory of a past dream in which the future was revealed. **(8)** _____ to say, few scientists **(9)** _____ these theories very seriously. Psychologists have made several **(10)** _____ to explain the phenomenon. Perhaps the most **(11)** _____ one involves a simple malfunction of the brain's electrical circuitry. What happens is this: the brain accidentally **(12)** _____ what you see as a memory *before* it is **(13)** _____ in the consciousness. So when, moments later, you actually **(14)** _____ conscious of the scene, you find that you **(15)** _____ have a memory of it deep in your mind.

0	**A** stage	**B** situation	**C** time	**D** period
1	**A** reaction	**B** sentiment	**C** taste	**D** sensation
2	**A** known	**B** called	**C** heard	**D** termed
3	**A** two	**B** else	**C** another	**D** more
4	**A** reason	**B** excuse	**C** answer	**D** explanation
5	**A** relating	**B** concerning	**C** referring	**D** owing
6	**A** far	**B** gone	**C** long	**D** lost
7	**A** maintain	**B** regard	**C** reply	**D** express
8	**A** Doubtless	**B** Only	**C** Without	**D** Needless
9	**A** accept	**B** take	**C** have	**D** hold
10	**A** attempts	**B** experiments	**C** Cries	**D** steps

11	**A** normal	**B** true	**C** right	**D** reasonable
12	**A** puts	**B** stores	**C** makes	**D** moves
13	**A** registered	**B** written	**C** signed	**D** listed
14	**A** come	**B** stay	**C** become	**D** be
15	**A** momentarily	**B** still	**C** just	**D** already

8 Read the text below and look carefully at each line. If the line is correct put a tick (✔). If a line has a word which should not be there, write the word. There are two examples, (0) and (00).

Modern life

0	My life is very different from that of my grandparents'	✔
00	generation. Some of things are better today and other	*of*
1	things are too worse. I am glad that we have TV today,	_____
2	because I think that life might be a bit boring without	_____
3	having it. I also like cars, computers, and video games.	_____
4	I think young people are have more fun today than	_____
5	young people of my grandparents' generation.	_____
6	However, there they are also a lot of bad things about	_____
7	life today. For our example, my grandparents did not	_____
8	have to live out with pollution when they were	_____
9	the younger. They could breathe clean air when	_____
10	they walked in the streets. Also, there was less	_____
11	crime made in those days. My grandparents did not	_____
12	have to worry about them being burgled or mugged	_____
13	in the same way as we worry today. Nevertheless,	_____
14	I am glad that I am young today, because I think so	_____
15	that the advantages outweigh the disadvantages.	_____

Travellers' tales

Compound adjectives

There are many ways of forming compound adjectives.

- To form compound adjectives of time or measurement we use a number and a singular noun, joined together with a hyphen.

   A ***three-day*** *course* (a course which lasts three days)
   A ***four-mile*** *walk* (a walk which is four miles long)

- Other compound adjectives can be formed by combining nouns, adjectives or adverbs with participles (or-*ed* words which look like participles).

   A ***radio-controlled*** *boat* (a boat which is controlled by radio-waves)
   A ***sad-looking*** *baby* (a baby who looks sad)
   A ***happily-married*** *woman* (a woman who is happy with her husband)
   A ***blue-eyed*** *boy* (a boy with blue eyes)
   A ***style-conscious*** *Englishwoman*
   An ***over-ambitious*** *enterprise*
   A ***well-behaved*** *child*
   A ***badly-injured*** *footballer*

1 Complete the second sentence using a compound adjective.

1 The child behaves well. He is a <u>*well-behaved child.*</u>

2 That man dresses in a scruffy manner. He is a _____.

3 This film star is very conscious of his image. This film star is very_____.

4 It takes five minutes to walk from my house to your house. It is a _____ from my house to your house.

5 They planned the attack in a very clever way. It was a very _____.

6 My cat has got short legs. It is a _____.

7 That woman always looks rather angry. She is a rather _____.

8 Her degree course took four years to complete. It was a _____.

9 What is the name of that perfume that smells horrible? What is the name of that _____?

10 Only members who carry their cards are allowed inside. Only _____ are allowed inside.

2 Read the text and decide which answer A, B, C or D best fits each space.

Conventional and Natural Medicine

Medical science has made enormous **(0)** _D_ in the twentieth century. Most of the great 'killer' diseases have been **(1)** _____, and almost every day a new drug appears on the market. But the medical profession is **(2)** _____ a crisis of confidence. Surveys **(3)** _____ that less than 40% of people really trust their family doctor. People are **(4)** _____ away from conventional medicine to look for alternative **(5)** _____ of treatment.

The main reason for this is that conventional medicine has **(6)** _____ to satisfy the needs of the **(7)** _____ of people. In spite of the apparent progress made by medical science, we are actually less **(8)** _____ than our parents or grandparents.

Medical students are taught that diseases are **(9)** _____ by germs, viruses and toxins. Therefore treatment must **(10)** _____ on attacking these things. The mind and the emotions are not thought to play any **(11)** _____ in the disease process. But people who practise 'natural' medicine **(12)** _____ with this principle, and try to treat the whole person. They believe that personality and lifestyle are important when considering a patient's **(13)** _____ health.

Some conventional doctors are beginning to **(14)** _____ that there is a lot of truth in these ideas, and believe that natural medicine can be a valuable aid. Others **(15)** _____ regard it as a dangerous threat to their profession.

	A	B	C	D
0	**A** steps	**B** distances	**C** increases	**D** advances
1	**A** won	**B** defeated	**C** erased	**D** broken
2	**A** experiencing	**B** holding	**C** bearing	**D** living
3	**A** indicate	**B** lead	**C** describe	**D** point
4	**A** growing	**B** taking	**C** turning	**D** coming
5	**A** ways	**B** makes	**C** forms	**D** fashions
6	**A** missed	**B** stopped	**C** lost	**D** failed
7	**A** lot	**B** majority	**C** most	**D** largest
8	**A** healthy	**B** nutritious	**C** fine	**D** wholesome
9	**A** caused	**B** made	**C** brought	**D** involved
10	**A** aim	**B** function	**C** concentrate	**D** try
11	**A** game	**B** piece	**C** part	**D** action
12	**A** reject	**B** dislike	**C** object	**D** disagree
13	**A** normal	**B** typical	**C** common	**D** general
14	**A** recognise	**B** observe	**C** view	**D** know
15	**A** still	**B** yet	**C** but	**D** even

Transport prepositions: *by, on* and *in*

By is used to talk about the method of travel. It is not used before an article or possessive pronoun:
   by train, by car, by bus, by plane, by taxi, by bicycle, by helicopter, by land, by sea, by air (BUT: on foot).

On is also used to talk about the method of travel, but it is used before an article or possessive:
   on the train, on a bus, on a plane, on my bicycle, on his horse, on the boat.

In is used in the same way as *on*, but with cars and taxis: *in the taxi, in your car.*

3 Underline the correct preposition.

1 I saw him riding into town <u>on</u>/by his bicycle yesterday.

2 He'd rather go *on/by* bus than drive there himself.

3 She sent him home *in/by* a taxi.

4 That's much too far to travel *on/in* foot.

5 Did you take the tunnel to France, or did you go *on/in* the ferry?

6 She rode through town *on/by* her horse.

7 Let's go home *in/by* taxi - I can't be bothered to walk.

8 She sometimes gets sick when travelling *on/by* sea.

9 He flies round the world *in/by* his own private jet.

10 The quickest way to get there is *on/by* air.

4 Complete the second sentence so that it has a similar meaning to the first sentence. Use the word in bold and other words. Use between two and five words.

1 Air travel frightens many people.

plane

Many people find travelling _____ frightening.

2 The train is the quickest way to get to London from here.

on

The quickest way to get to London from here _____ train.

3 Sometimes it is quicker to walk than to drive to work.

foot

Sometimes it is quicker to go to _____ than to drive.

4 The bicycle is my favourite form of transport

by

I prefer _____ than any other way.

5 We used the car that belonged to my uncle to drive to Wales.

drove

We _____ my uncle's car.

5 Read the text below and look carefully at each line. If the line is correct put a tick (✔). If a line has a word which should not be there, write the word. There are two examples, (0) and (00).

Travel

0	One of my main ambitions is to travel around the	✔
00	world, visiting to as many countries as possible. I	*to*
1	think that travelling is a very good way to learn	_____
2	about the life. It is important to understand that	_____
3	there are many of different ways to live, and that our	_____
4	own culture is not necessarily being better than other	_____
5	cultures. On the other hand, I realise that it is very	_____
6	hard to get to know that a foreign country well if	_____
7	you are just passing through as a tourist. That is	_____
8	why I would try this to talk to the local people of the	_____
9	country I was visiting. If we did not have understand	_____
10	each other's language, then maybe we could talk in	_____
11	English. I would not like to travel on my own self	_____
12	because that could be lonely, or even dangerous. I	_____
13	would take and my best friend with me. The only	_____
14	problem I have about travelling around the world is	_____
15	money. I would have to save for years so to be able to	_____
	afford such an expensive holiday!	_____

The Future

The present simple is used to talk about a timetabled future or a fixed future which we cannot change.

> The sun **sets** at 8.32 this evening. (Nothing can be done to change this)
> Our plane **arrives** at 7.15 tomorrow. (It is timetabled)

The present continuous is used to talk about plans or arrangements in the near future.

> I'**m meeting** Sue this evening. (It is arranged)

The *be going to* + infinitive future is used:

- to talk about future intentions concerning ourselves.

> I'**m going to be** a fireman when I grow up. (It is my intention, but it has not been arranged)
> She **is going to look** for another job. (She intends to)

- to predict that something will happen, because there is evidence that it will.

> Look! That cat **is going to kill** that bird. (The cat is about to jump on the unsuspecting bird)
> Your dad **is going to be** very angry when he sees this. (I know your father, and I know how he will react)

6 Put the verbs in brackets into the correct future tense.

1 Hurry up! The plane _arrives_ (arrive) at 7.30.

2 There's no point in running now. We _____ (miss) the bus anyway.

3 Yes, I'll come out this evening. I _____ (not/work).

4 You can relax. The match _____ (not/start) until four o'clock.

5 I _____ (go) to the market this afternoon. Do you want anything?

6 Are you OK, Donna? You look like you _____ (faint).

7 You realise that the boss _____ (not/like) this, don't you?

8 I _____ (cook) dinner this evening - as usual.

9 She _____ (look) for a new flat next year.

10 Don't worry. The shops _____ (not/close) until eight o'clock tonight.

7 Complete the second sentence so that it has a similar meaning to the first sentence. Use the word in bold and other words. Use between two and five words.

1 Simon intends to join the police force when he leaves school.
   is
   When Simon leaves school _____ the police force.

2 He is such a bad driver that he is almost certain to have an accident soon.
   going
   I think _____ an accident soon, because he is such a bad driver.

3 The departure time for the train is 8.35.
   at
   The train _____ 8.35.

4 I have arranged to meet my bank manager in the near future.
   am
   I _____ soon.

5 They say that if the cows are lying down, rain will soon follow.
   is
   They say that if the cows are lying down, it means that _____ rain.

6 What do you intend to do with all that money?
   are
   What _____ with all that money?

7 He has decided never to drink whisky again.
   is
   He _____ whisky again.

8 We have not arranged to do anything in particular this weekend.
   are
   We _____ anything in particular this weekend.

9 I do not intend to help him, even if he pays me.
   am
   Even if he pays me, I _____ him.

10 The film is scheduled to begin at four o'clock.
    not
    The film _____ until four o'clock.

So/Such...that

So can be used

- like *very* to emphasise adjectives or adverbs:

   *This child is **so** quiet.* (very quiet)
   *He drives **so** dangerously.* (very dangerously)

- to link adjectives or adverbs to a result clause using *that*:

   *This child is **so** quiet **that** I often forget he's here.*
   *He drives **so** dangerously **that** it frightens me.*

Such a can be used

- in a similar way to emphasise adjectives (but not adverbs), and link them to a result clause:

   *This is **such a** quiet child **that** I often forget he's here.*
   *He is **such a** dangerous driver **that** it frightens me.*

Such is followed by *a* except when the adjective refers to an uncountable noun or the plural of a countable noun:

   *It was **such** delicious soup **that** I had two bowls.*
   *They were **such** cheap tickets **that** I bought one for everyone.*

So can be used with

- quantifiers like *many, much, little, few:*

   *There were **so few** people at the party **that** we went home.*
   *We had **so much** to eat **that** we felt ill.*

Such can only be used with quantifiers which take the indefinite article like *a lot, a small/large number, a lack:*

   *There was **such a lack** of interest **that** we called the trip off.*
   *We had **such a lot** of fun **that** we're going back next year.*

8 Fill in the gaps with *so, such* or *such a*.

1 The bread was _so_ fresh that it was still warm.

2 I'm sure Philip will pass his exams. He is _____ clever boy.

3 We all had headaches after the concert because the music was _____ loud.

4 I don't know how you can afford to buy _____ expensive clothes.

5 Sally speaks _____ softly that I sometimes have difficulty hearing her.

6 The house cost _____ huge amount of money that we couldn't even consider buying it.

7 Why do _____ few people take an interest in local politics these days?

8 Melanie is _____ pretty that she could be a model.

9 It was _____ strongly-flavoured cheese that I couldn't eat it.

10 He seldom left the house because he was _____ afraid of dogs.

9 Complete the second sentence so that it has a similar meaning to the first sentence. Use the word in bold and other words. Use between two and five words.

1 There was such a lack of food in the house that we had to spend over £100 at the supermarket.

little

There _____ in the house that we had to spend over £100 at the supermarket.

2 This boy writes so well that he could be an author when he grows up.

good

This boy _____ that he could be an author when he grows up.

3 He is a good climber because his arms are so strong.

got

He is a good climber because he _____ arms.

4 Lucy makes friends easily because she has got so much confidence.

is

Lucy _____ that she makes friends easily.

5 So many people wanted to go on the trip that we had to hire another bus.

number

We had to hire another bus because _____ of people wanted to go on the trip.

6 She cried with happiness.

so

She _____ that she cried.

7 Les is such a bad pianist that no one can bear to listen to him.

piano

Les plays _____ that no one can bear to listen to him.

8 I am so rich that I could buy two Ferraris if I wanted to.

much

I _____ that I could buy two Ferraris if I wanted to.

9 In her anger she threw the plate against the wall.

angry

She _____ that she threw the plate against the wall.

10 There is a lot to do, and not much time in which to do it.

little

So ~~few~~ _____-_____ time!

10 Read the text below and think of the word which best fits each space. Use only one word in each space.

Edinburgh

Edinburgh, the capital city of Scotland, **(0)** _is_ regarded by many people **(1)**_____ the most beautiful city in Europe. Whether or **(2)**_____ that is true, no visitor can fail to **(3)**_____ impressed by its dramatic surroundings, its magnificent buildings, or its dark stone churches.

Edinburgh Castle dominates **(4)**_____ city centre. Built in the eleventh century, **(5)**_____ sits high on a rock. The Old Town developed from this point, stretching down the slope to form what is **(6)**_____ as the Royal Mile. This street remains **(7)**_____ of the city's main tourist attractions, with Holyroodhouse (a royal palace) at the lower end, and the castle at the top.

The New Town **(8)**_____ built in the eighteenth century in order to cope **(9)**_____ the increasing population of the city. It is located in the flat land to the north **(10)**_____ the castle. Before it was developed, **(11)**_____ competition was arranged for the best design. The Scottish architect, James Craig, won with a simple grid pattern of streets and squares.

But perhaps Edinburgh is most famous **(12)**_____ its annual International Festival of Music and Drama. This massive three-week event has been held every August **(13)**_____ 1947. It attracts thousands of theatre and music lovers, and hundreds of artists, from **(14)**_____ over the world. Not surprisingly, many Edinburgh locals take their holidays at this time - and go in **(15)**_____ of some peace and quiet!

Multi-word verbs

11 Use the correct form of the multi-word verbs below to rewrite the second sentence so that it means exactly the same as the first sentence.

call on	set off	run out	check out
take off	take part	catch out	call for

1 We **began our journey to** France on 1 April.

We _____.

2 Mr Thomas **paid the hotel bill and handed in his keys** this morning.

Mr Thomas _____.

3 Our supply of food **is almost gone**.

Our _____.

4 A lot of people were **put in a difficult situation** by the sudden fall in house prices.

The sudden fall in house prices _____.

5 Unfortunately, the song never really **became successful** in the United States.

Unfortunately, the song _____.

6 Why didn't you **visit** me when you were in town?

Why didn't you _____?

7 A great deal of strength and fitness **is needed** for rock-climbing.

Rock-climbing _____.

8 There was some fighting at the football match, but Gary did not **become involved**.

Gary did not _____.

Food for thought

Gerund and infinitive

Some verbs are followed by a gerund (-*ing* form). Here are a few of them:

> *admit appreciate avoid can't help can't stand consider delay deny detest discuss enjoy escape excuse face fancy feel like finish forgive give up imagine involve keep mention mind miss practise prevent put off resent resist risk suggest tolerate understand*

Some verbs are followed by the infinitive. Here are a few of them:

> *afford agree appear arrange ask attempt bear care choose consent dare decide expect fail happen help hesitate hope learn manage neglect offer plan prepare pretend promise refuse seem tend wish*

Some verbs can take either an -ing form or an infinitive without really altering the meaning. Here are some common ones:

> *begin (I **began feeling/to feel** ill after dinner.)*
> *continue (He **continued talking/to talk** all through the night.)*
> *intend (Do you **intend leaving/to leave** early today?)*
> *start (She **started learning/to learn** Spanish last year.)*

1 Put the verbs in brackets into the -*ing* form or the infinitive. Sometimes both are possible.

1 I really don't feel like *going* (go) to work today.

2 Did you manage _____ (finish) the project on time?

3 He crashed his car into a tree in order to avoid _____ (hit) a dog.

4 As soon as she started _____ (speak) I realised that she was not English.

5 Alison does not appear _____ (care) about whether she passes or fails.

6 I gave up _____ (ski) after one day because I kept _____ (fall) over.

7 Malcolm suggested _____ (dine) at the Hilton, but we could not afford _____ (eat) in such an expensive place.

8 Why did you refuse _____ (lend) Tony £50?

Because I didn't want to risk _____ (lose) it!

9 What do you intend _____ (do) when you finish college?

I fancy _____ (join) the Navy.

10 She agreed _____ (help) him in the garden, as long as it didn't involve _____ (get) her hands dirty.

2 Read the text below and look carefully at each line. If the line is correct put a tick (✔). If a line has a word which should not be there, write the word. There are two examples, (0) and (00).

Picnics

0	One of the most nicest ways to spend a summer	*most*
00	afternoon is to have a picnic. There is something	✔
1	about eating out of doors that it is very special. A	_____
2	barbecue can also be fun, but it is not like the same.	_____
3	A picnic involves in adventure and discovery, whereas	_____
4	most of people just have barbecues in their gardens	_____
5	or on their balconies. Of course, some things are	_____
6	essential if the picnic is going to be for an enjoyable	_____
7	experience. Firstly, the weather has to be sunny;	_____
8	not a many people enjoy eating sandwiches in the	_____
9	pouring rain! Secondly, the site must to be carefully	_____
10	chosen. Beaches, although they may sound	_____
11	attractive, are seldom ideal for not picnicking	_____
12	purposes because the sand will always finds its way	_____
13	into the food. In my opinion, the perfect picnic	_____
14	spot is in the mountains, next side to a river. Then,	_____
15	when the meal is been finished, you can just relax in	_____
	the sunshine, or go for a swim.	

Gerund and infinitive (continued)

Some verbs take either an *-ing* form or an infinitive, depending on the intended meaning. Here are the main ones:

- need
  1 *I **need to go** to the doctor.* (It is necessary for me to go.)
  2 *My hair **needs cutting**.* (It needs to be cut – passive meaning.)

- remember
  1 *Try to **remember to phone** me.* (The *to* infinitive refers to the future.)
  2 *Do you **remember going** to school for the first time?* (The *-ing* form refers to the past.)

- forget
  1 *I **forgot to tell** you about the party.* (The *to* infinitive refers to a future action from a past perspective.)
  2 *I'll never **forget flying** for the first time.* (The *-ing* form refers to a past action.)

- regret
  1 *I **regret to tell** you that you are very ill.* (The *to* infinitive refers to the present/immediate future.)
  2 *I **regret telling** you my secret.* (The *-ing* form refers to a past action.)

- stop
  1 *He **stopped to buy** some flowers.* (He stopped for a purpose.)
  2 *Will you **stop talking**, please.* (Will you finish; the *-ing* form is the object of the verb.)

- try
  1 *Why don't you **try to work** harder?* (Attempt, or make an effort.)
  2 *You should **try going** to bed earlier.* (Do it as an experiment.)

3 Put the verbs in brackets into the -*ing* form or the infinitive.

1 Jenny told me that she regrets _____ (shout) at you last night.

2 Oh no! I think I have forgotten _____ (lock) the door.

3 Did you remember _____ (phone) your mother on Mother's Day?

4 I wish the children would stop _____ (make) so much noise.

5 He needs _____ (go) to the hospital for tests.

6 We regret _____ (inform) you that we cannot offer you the job.

7 I stopped _____ (get) some petrol on my way home from work.

8 I do not remember _____ (give) you permission to use my car.

9 The baby won't stop _____ (cry). I think she needs _____ (feed).

10 Mary always forgets _____ (close) the fridge after she has used it.

Have you tried _____ (put) a notice up on the door?

4 Complete the second sentence so that it has a similar meaning to the first sentence. Use the word in bold and other words. Use between two and five words.

1 I will send you out of the classroom if you continue to make so much noise.
keep
If _____ so much noise, I will send you out of the classroom.

2 'Would you like to go fishing?' Tom asked me.
felt
Tom asked me if _____ fishing.

3 I wish I had not spent so much money last night.
regret
I _____ so much money last night.

4 He found it impossible to keep his good news secret from her.
resist
He could _____ his good news.

5 I will always remember the first time I met Martha.
never
I _____ Martha for the first time.

6 'No, I did not shoot Mr Fordham', said Robby.
denied
Robby _____ Mr Fordham.

7 Could you open the window, please?
mind
Would _____, please?

8 I got the impression that Jenkins was not trying very hard.
   seem
   Jenkins _____ trying very hard.

9 Why don't you ask him if he needs any help?
   offer
   Why don't _____ him?

10 We tried not to laugh at his new haircut, but it was impossible.
    help
    We _____ at his new haircut.

5 Read the text and decide which answer A, B, C or D best fits each space.

Salt

Salt is **(0)** _C_ to life. At one time it was considered so valuable that it was **(1)** _____ worshipped as a god. Roman soldiers **(2)** _____ to be paid 'salt money', which is where the word 'salary' originated **(3)** _____. Nowadays, however, salt is so common that few people even **(4)** _____ to think about it. But perhaps they **(5)** _____.

The human body needs so little salt to **(6)** _____ that it is very easy to consume too much of it. An excess of salt in the diet can **(7)** _____ to high blood pressure, which in turn can **(8)** _____ the risk of heart disease. Cooking with salt also reduces the nutritional quality of the food. For example, spinach boiled in salted water **(9)** _____ 50% of its iron, compared to only 19% when boiled in salt-**(10)** _____ water. Many people have the habit of **(11)** _____ salt to their food when they are at the table. Some even do this **(12)** _____ they have tasted the food. This is one of the reasons why the **(13)** _____ person in Britain eats two and a half to three teaspoons of salt every day. The **(14)** _____ recommended dose is one and a half, and the **(15)** _____ dose is just half a teaspoon.

		A		B		C		D
0	**A**	compulsory	**B**	needed	**C**	essential	**D**	absolute
1	**A**	actually	**B**	really	**C**	currently	**D**	factually
2	**A**	were	**B**	would	**C**	once	**D**	used
3	**A**	out	**B**	from	**C**	off	**D**	to
4	**A**	mind	**B**	worry	**C**	bother	**D**	dare
5	**A**	ought	**B**	should	**C**	would	**D**	had
6	**A**	survive	**B**	last	**C**	keep	**D**	maintain
7	**A**	bring	**B**	reach	**C**	end	**D**	lead
8	**A**	lift	**B**	increase	**C**	rise	**D**	grow
9	**A**	drops	**B**	kills	**C**	loses	**D**	throws
10	**A**	free	**B**	clean	**C**	empty	**D**	clear
11	**A**	putting	**B**	mixing	**C**	including	**D**	adding
12	**A**	without	**B**	instead	**C**	before	**D**	prior
13	**A**	medium	**B**	average	**C**	common	**D**	usual
14	**A**	top	**B**	extreme	**C**	maximum	**D**	most
15	**A**	ideal	**B**	superior	**C**	good	**D**	excellent

Too/enough

Too is used before adjectives, quantifiers and adverbs. It means 'excessively' or 'more than is necessary'.

> It is much **too hot** in here.
> There are **too many** people in this room.
> He drinks **too much**.
> You eat **too quickly**.

Enough is used after adjectives and adverbs, or directly before nouns. It means 'to the necessary degree' or 'sufficient'.

> This water isn't **cold enough**.
> We have **enough money** now.

6 Complete the dialogues with *too* or *enough* and the word in brackets.

1 I've got stomach-ache.

I'm not surprised. You ate your dinner *too quickly* (quickly).

2 It's _____ (cold) in my room.

Why don't you turn the heating on then?

3 Do you want to play football this weekend?

I can't. I'm not _____ (fit).

4 It wasn't a very good party, was it?

No. Barry didn't invite _____ (people).

5 Did you buy the Mercedes?

No. It cost _____ (much).

6 I'm surprised that Colin is going to university.

Me too. I didn't think he was _____ (clever).

7 Have you got _____ (money) for the bus home?

No. Can I borrow some?

8 There isn't _____ (room) for everyone to go in my car.

No, there are _____ (many) of us. Some of us will have to get a taxi.

9 Why didn't you get the job? Were you _____ (young)?

No. It was because I didn't have _____ (qualifications).

10 When will you be _____ (well) to come back to work?

Next week. But the doctor says I mustn't work _____ (hard).

Zero and first conditionals

The zero conditional is formed with *if* or *when* + present tense in the conditional clause, and a present tense in the result clause.

It is used to talk about things which always or usually happen in a certain situation.

> *If you **boil** soup, it **spoils** the flavour.* (It always happens.)
> *You **get** one point **when** you **answer** a question correctly.* (These are the rules.)

The first conditional is formed with *if* or *unless* + present tense in the conditional clause, and the simple future tense (*will* + infinitive) in the result clause. It is used to talk about things which will, or will not, happen in a probable, or real, future situation.

> *If you **cook** dinner, I **will clean** the bathroom.*
> *I **will call** you if I **need** any help.* (It is a real possibility that I will need help.)

Unless refers to a negative condition. It means 'except on the condition, or under the circumstance that'.

> *I'll meet you at five o'clock, **unless** you change your mind.* (Provided you do not change your mind.)
> ***Unless** you behave yourself, I will punish you.* (If you do not behave yourself.)

7 Put the verbs in brackets into the correct tense.

1 If you pick me up from work today, I _____ (buy) you a drink.

2 You _____ (get) a free pen when you spend more than £20 at this bookshop.

3 I _____ (meet) you in the square, unless you'd prefer to meet somewhere else.

4 When autumn comes, the leaves _____ (fall) from the trees.

5 He works flexible hours; if there is not much to do, he _____ (come) home early.

6 Unless you _____ (apologise), I'll never speak to you again.

7 Shortly after a bee stings you, it _____ (die).

8 She _____ (not/come) to your party if you don't invite her.

9 If you buy a car, I _____ (sell) my motorbike.

10 _____ (you/give) Sally my address if you see her?

11 The rules of this club are very strict; if you _____ (break) them, you are asked to leave.

12 He will never be promoted unless he _____ (learn) to be more polite to the customers.

13 If you really want me to, I _____ (take) the dog to the vet.

14 This machine is easy to operate; the engine _____ (start) when you press the green button, and _____ (stop) when you press the red one.

The *will* future

This future form is formed with *will* + infinitive. It is used to make offers, promises, on-the-spot decisions and personal predictions.

> *I'**ll have** the chicken Kiev, please.* (I've just decided.)
> *I **will write** to you every day.* (I promise.)
> *I'**ll give** you a hand with that.* (It is an offer.)
> *He **will/will not be** happy to hear from you.* (It's a prediction.)

8 Underline the word or phrase which completes each sentence correctly.

1 Where is the bathroom? I think *I'll/I'm going to* be sick.

2 Sharon *will be/is being* happy to hear your news.

3 Wait! *I'll give/I'm giving* you my number in case you need me.

4 He *will meet/is meeting* me at 1 o'clock.

5 I have decided that I *don't speak/am not going to speak* to him again.

6 Excuse me. What time *will/does* the train from Edinburgh arrive?

7 I predict that Sam *won't get/isn't getting* the job - he's too unreliable.

8 I don't feel like going out tonight. I think *I'll just go/I'm just going* to bed.

9 Judy can't come away with us next weekend. *She'll work/ She's working.*

10 I promise *I'll bring/I'm going to bring* you a present from America.

9 Read the text below and think of the word which best fits each space. Use only one word in each space.

Stuck in a lift

To be stuck in a lift **(0)** *for* any length of time is a nightmare **(1)**_____ true for many people. So pity poor Graham Coates **(2)**_____ was trapped inside one for *three whole days* ! One Saturday morning in 1986, he decided to go to work at his office, which was **(3)**_____ the second floor of a large office block. Somewhere **(4)**_____ the first and second floor, the lift stopped. He pushed the alarm bell but, as **(5)**_____ was the weekend, the office block was empty. The noise **(6)**_____ not be heard from outside the building.

He tried shouting, but no one was able to hear that **(7)**_____. Eventually, he decided **(8)**_____ he would just have to wait. Nobody reported him missing because he was living with **(9)**_____ parents at the time and he often spent weekends away **(10)**_____ home. He began to get thirsty, and then hungry. By Sunday he was dreaming of long cool drinks, and the lovely meal that people **(11)**_____ be enjoying in the pub **(12)**_____ he worked at weekends.

Monday was a national holiday, so it was not **(13)**_____ Tuesday morning that he was rescued by his boss. By that time he was very weak and ill. He had to have several days **(14)**_____ work, and still gets headaches even today. Now he refuses to enter any lift which does not **(15)**_____ a telephone installed!

Defining and non-defining relative clauses

A defining relative clause identifies the noun, giving necessary information about it. It is not enclosed by commas.

*Children **who eat too many sweets** get bad teeth.*

A non-defining relative clause gives extra information about the noun, not essential to the meaning of the main clause. It is enclosed by commas.

*My Mum, **who was born in Wales**, makes great chocolate cake.*

Sometimes the only way to tell whether a clause is defining or non-defining is by the presence or absence of commas. Compare these two sentences:

a   *The guests, who ate the prawn cocktail for starters, were sick.*
b   *The guests who ate the prawn cocktail for starters were sick.*

In sentence **a**, all the guests were sick; the non-defining relative clause between the commas gives us extra information, and the sentence meaning would not alter without it:

The guests were sick.

In sentence **b**, however, the defining relative clause tells us specifically *which* guests were sick, ie only those unfortunate enough to have eaten the prawn cocktail.

10 Underline the correct relative pronoun, and add commas where necessary.

1 My uncle, *who*/that is in the army, bought me a gun for Christmas.

2 The building *which/where* I'm working in has no heating.

3 Mrs Phillips *which/whose* daughter is an actress owns five televisions.

4 Only a few people *who/which* play the lottery actually win anything.

5 World War 1 *which/that* lasted four years was fought mainly in Europe.

6 The man *who/which* lives downstairs from me likes heavy metal music.

7 Steven lives in a town *which/where* has very few restaurants.

8 We are going to spend a week in Prague *which/where* our friends live.

9 Do you remember the time *when/where* we got lost in the woods?

10 The vases *which/who* were not packed properly were damaged in the post.

11 Use the word at the end of each line to form a word that fits in the space on the same line.

The microwave

The microwave oven has **(0)** *revolutionised* the way   **REVOLUTION**
food is cooked both at home and within the food **(1)**_____ **PREPARE**
industry. Although it met with the **(2)**_____ of many **DISAPPROVE**
top chefs when it was invented, it is becoming an **(3)**_____ **INCREASE**
common sight in many restaurant kitchens. So what are its
advantages? Firstly, there is a huge **(4)**_____ in the **REDUCE**
amount of time needed to prepare each dish. Secondly, it is
a very **(5)**_____ way to cook, because microwaves are **HYGIENE**
easy to clean, and the high temperatures involved **(6)**_____ **MINIMUM**
the risk of **(7)**_____ infection. Finally, microwave ovens **BACTERIA**
are very **(8)**_____ to the busy professional person who **ATTRACT**
lives alone. The **(9)**_____ of a 'microwave dinner' is **CONVENIENT**
(10)_____ to someone who does not wish to waste their **RESIST**
time sweating over a hot cooker!

High-tech horizons

The passive

The passive is formed with the object + the verb *to be* (in any tense) + past participle.

> *My **computer was stolen**.* (Somebody stole my computer.)

The passive is used
- to describe a process:

> The ***bread is put*** *in the oven and **baked** for 20 minutes.*

- when the action is more important than who does it:

> *The **TV is being repaired** this afternoon.* (It does not matter who is repairing it.)

- when we do not know, do not care, or do not want to say who does the action:

> *The **money has been returned**.* (But it would be indiscreet to say who has returned it.)

The *agent* is the person or thing that does the action. It is only included if it adds important information:

> *This house was built **by my grandfather**.* (The fact that my grandfather built this house is interesting.)
> *The thief was arrested outside the supermarket.* (We do not say *by the police* because that is obvious, and does not add important information.)

---

1   Change the following sentences from active to passive. Omit the agent if it is not needed.

1   Someone has returned the stolen cash.

   The stolen cash has been returned.

2   They will not send you any money until next month.

   You _____.

3   Aunt Dorothy is looking after the children.

   _____.

4   Has anyone informed you about the change of plan?

   _____?

5   My brother stole my wallet.

   _____.

6   You must add milk and flour to the eggs.

   _____.

7   Do you know who wrote *The Sting*?

   Do _____?

8 His father didn't give him any encouragement.

He _____.

9 We suddenly realised that someone had tricked us.

We _____.

10 Inspector Jarvis was interviewing the suspect at 10 o'clock this morning.

_____.

2 Complete the second sentence so that it has a similar meaning to the first sentence. Use the word in bold and other words. Use between two and five words.

1 Mark's main rival beat him in the final.

beaten

Mark _____ by his main rival.

2 Their wedding was not in a church.

were

They _____ in a church.

3 Sheffield is my place of birth.

born

I _____ Sheffield.

4 We were warned not to go out at night.

us

They _____ not to go out at night.

5 Who invented the mobile phone?

was

Who_____ by?

6 Mr Hopkins is the owner of that blue Toyota.

by

That blue Toyota _____ Mr Hopkins.

7 A new hospital is being built in town.

building

They _____ in town.

8 Why did nobody tell me about the accident?

not

Why _____ about the accident?

9 She was wearing leather gloves.

of

The gloves she was wearing _____ leather.

10 You work for IBM, don't you?

are

You _____, aren't you?

3 Read the text and decide which answer A, B, C or D best fits each space.

Listening

Human beings have a strong need to **(0)** __B__ their experiences and problems into words. That is why everyone **(1)** _____ a 'friendly ear' - someone who is **(2)** ____ to listen to their troubles and joys. But few people **(3)** ____ what a complex skill listening is. To be a good listener requires great **(4)** ____ of concentration, which can only be gained through practice.

There are two reasons why listening is often such hard **(5)** ____ . The first is simply that people much **(6)** ____ to speak. How often have you **(7)** ____ what someone has said because you were thinking about what you were going to say in **(8)** ____? The second reason is that people speak too slowly. The average speed is about 125 words per minute, **(9)** ____ is not fast enough for the human brain. It **(10)** ____ too much time for the concentration to fail, as the brain tries to **(11)** ____ itself busy with other, irrelevant thoughts.

Next time you are in a listening **(12)** ____, try to predict what the speaker is going to say. Ask yourself questions about what is being said, and **(13)** ____ if the speaker answers them. Finally, make quick summaries in your head of the main **(14)** ____ that have been made. All of these things will **(15)** ____ you to concentrate and make you a better listener.

0	**A** say	**B** put	**C** tell	**D** place
1	**A** approves	**B** applauds	**C** appreciates	**D** attracts
2	**A** agreed	**B** wanting	**C** capable	**D** willing
3	**A** realise	**B** believe	**C** relate	**D** detect
4	**A** forces	**B** skills	**C** powers	**D** strengths
5	**A** job	**B** work	**C** task	**D** act
6	**A** sooner	**B** rather	**C** prefer	**D** like
7	**A** lost	**B** dropped	**C** slipped	**D** missed
8	**A** report	**B** answer	**C** reply	**D** turn
9	**A** that	**B** what	**C** this	**D** which
10	**A** lets	**B** allows	**C** makes	**D** admits
11	**A** keep	**B** stop	**C** maintain	**D** hold
12	**A** station	**B** circumstance	**C** atmosphere	**D** situation
13	**A** look	**B** watch	**C** see	**D** tell
14	**A** marks	**B** points	**C** topics	**D** ideas
15	**A** aid	**B** serve	**C** give	**D** help

Predictions: *will* or *going to*?

The future with *will* is used for predictions when we are giving our personal opinion of what will happen.

> *I think you* **will enjoy** *this film.* (It is my opinion.)

The *going to* future is used when there is evidence that something will definitely happen.

> *My aunt* **is going to have** *a baby.* (She is eight months pregnant – the evidence is there.)

4   Complete the dialogues with *will* or *going to*, and one of the verbs below.

enjoy	know	keep	die	take off
redecorate	crash	own	steal	help

1   Why do you want me to come to the club with you?

Because I think *you'll enjoy* it.

2   What is the capital of Peru?

Why don't you ask Peter? He _____.

3   Why have the Dixons bought so much paint?

They _____ their house.

4   Look! Number seven has lost control of his car.

Oh no! He _____ !

5   The plane is moving onto the runway now.

Yes. It _____ in a minute.

6   Do you have any predictions for the future, Professor?

By the end of the century, 80% of households _____ a computer.

7   Have you decided what to do with that money you found?

Yes. I _____ it.

8   I'm having trouble with this exercise.

Tell Gina. She _____ you.

9   How is he, doctor?

I'm afraid there is no hope. He _____.

10   Shall I park the car here?

No, not here. Someone _____ it.

5   Read the text below and think of the word which best fits each space. Use only one word in each space.

Passive smoking

Even **(0)** *if* you have never touched a cigarette in your life you are still **(1)**_____ risk from smoking-related diseases if you live, work or travel with smokers. When smokers and non-smokers share the **(2)**_____ room, the non-smokers cannot avoid breathing in some **(3)**_____ the smokers' tobacco smoke. This is called 'passive smoking'.

People's awareness of the dangers of smoking **(4)**_____ increased a lot in recent years. More people **(5)**_____ giving up than ever before. Smoking has **(6)**_____ banned from most forms of public transport, and nearly all public buildings have **(7)**_____ 'smoke-free zones'. However, in the workplace many people are still exposed **(8)**_____ the danger and discomfort of passive smoking.

(9)_____ are many benefits to an employer taking action to create a smoke-free environment. For a **(10)**_____, the company has a better, cleaner image. Secondly, the workforce are healthier and happier, less likely to take time **(11)**_____ due to illness, and more likely to stay with the company. Thirdly, cleaning costs are greatly reduced for **(12)**_____ the employer and the employee, neither of

(13)_____ have to go home in clothes that stink of smoke.

When a non-smoking policy is first introduced, there is usually some protest (14)_____ the smokers. But eventually even the smokers come to appreciate (15)_____ benefits of working in a smoke-free environment, and many are encouraged to give up smoking altogether.

So and *nor*

When agreeing with a positive statement, we use *so* + auxiliary + subject.

> *I love pizza.* – **So do I**.
> *I can understand this.* – **So can my Dad.**

When agreeing with a negative statement, we use *nor/neither* + auxiliary + subject.

> *I don't like computers.* – **Neither/Nor does Sara.**
> *I can't drive.* – **Neither/Nor can I**.

6   Agree with the following statements using *so* or *neither/nor*, and the subject in brackets.

1   Norman can't ride a bike. – *Neither/Nor can I* (I)

2   We love dancing. – _____. (we)

3   Barry should go out more often. – _____. (Gordon)

4   You can't speak Spanish. – _____. (you)

5   I hate flying. – _____. (I)

6   They couldn't find the concert hall. – _____. (we)

7   I might go fishing this weekend. – _____. (Simon)

8   She doesn't want to study law. – _____. (I)

9   He will be surprised to hear that. – _____. (she)

10   I'm going to bed early tonight. – _____.(I)

The second conditional

The second conditional is formed with *if* + past tense in the conditional clause, and *would* + infinitive in the result clause.

It is used to talk about imaginary situations and their imaginary results. Although the past tense is used, we are actually talking about the present.

> **If I won** *the lottery,* **I would buy** *my parents a new house.* (But I haven't won the lottery.)
> *I* **would be** *very surprised* **if she passed** *her driving test.* (She has not got her driving licence now, and probably never will.)
> *This hat* **would fit** *me* **if my head was** *smaller.* (But, obviously, my head will stay the same size.)

7 Complete the second sentence so that it has a similar meaning to the first sentence. Use the word in bold and other words. Use between two and five words.

1 I only go to work because I need the money.
   not
   If _____ the money, I would not go to work.

2 I think it is unlikely that Liverpool will win the championship.
   surprised
   I _____ if Liverpool won the championship.

3 The only time she speaks to her boss is when she has to.
   never
   She _____ to her boss if she didn't have to.

4 They only complain because they are treated badly.
   well
   If_____, they wouldn't complain.

5 She doesn't have any friends, so she feels lonely.
   some
   If _____, she wouldn't feel lonely.

6 I don't see her very often because she lives in Australia.
   more
   I _____ if she didn't live in Australia.

7 The reason he isn't going to buy the car is because it is too expensive.
   cheaper
   If _____ he would buy it.

8 They only punish you because you are bad.
   good
   If you _____, they wouldn't punish you.

9 She won't invite you to dinner because she doesn't know you well enough.
   better
   If_____, she would invite you to dinner.

10 My dog has got short legs, so it can't run very fast.
   able
   My dog _____ to run faster if it had longer legs.

8 Put the verbs in brackets into the correct tense.

1 I *would write* (write) to her if I knew her address.

2 When the sun _____ (shine) I like to lie in the garden.

3 If you _____ (move) to China you would have to learn to speak the language.

4 We _____ (grow) our own vegetables if we had a garden.

5 What will you do if the boat _____ (sink)?

6 If I showed you how to open the safe, _____ (you/promise) not to tell anyone?

7 She _____ (not/buy) it if she didn't think she needed it.

8 If the police come looking for you I _____ (say) you have left the country.

9 I wouldn't mind living in this city if the traffic _____ (not/be) so bad.

10 The salad _____ (taste) better if you added some garlic.

9 Read the text below and look carefully at each line. If the line is correct put a tick (✓). If a line has a word which should not be there, write the word. There are two examples, (0) and (00).

Television

0	Some people think that the television it is the	*it*
00	most terrible invention of the twentieth century.	✓
1	They believe that it kills conversation within the	_____
2	family, exposes children to the violent images,	_____
3	and discourages from reading and thinking. I think	_____
4	that there is some truth in what they do say, but	_____
5	I also think that they are ignoring the good	_____
6	aspects of television. Without no TV we would	_____
7	know then much less about what was happening	_____
8	in the world. The speed and efficiency of a TV	_____
9	technology means that when something happens	_____
10	on the other side of the world, we can to hear about	_____
11	it within hours. I think that TV also promotes for	_____
12	understanding between different cultures. Before	_____
13	that it was invented very few people got the	_____
14	chance to see other parts of the world, or other	_____
15	ways of life. I think so the educational advantages	_____
	of TV outweigh the disadvantages.	

Working out

1 Use the word at the end of each line to form a word that fits in the space on the same line.

Exercise - the case against

We are always being told about the **(0)** _beneficial_ effects of   **BENEFIT**

regular and **(1)** _____ physical exercise. But how often do   **VIGOUR**

you hear people talking about the **(2)** _____ aspects of this   **HARM**

modern **(3)** _____ with health and fitness?   **OBSESS**

It is time people realised that exercise is an **(4)** _____. The   **ADDICT**

act of exercising releases a chemical in the brain which has

the **(5)** _____ effect of making you feel both relaxed   **PLEASURE**

and **(6)** _____. It is, in fact, a drug. That is why real   **ENERGY**

fitness-freaks feel the need to work out **(7)** _____ often,   **INCREASE**

and become **(8)** _____ and depressed if they are kept   **NERVE**

away from the gym for too long.

So before you sign up for a year's **(9)** _____ at your local   **MEMBER**

health club, ask yourself if you are really **(10)** _____ to   **WILL**

sacrifice your freedom and self-respect for the sake of 'fitness'.

Present perfect continuous

The present perfect continuous is formed with _to have_ + _been_ + present participle (_-ing_ form). It is used

- to emphasise that an action which started in the past has either continued up to the present, or very recently finished:

   She **has been cooking** this meal all afternoon. (It is still this afternoon and she is still cooking.)
   I **have been studying** for this test all morning. (I started studying when I got up this morning, and I am now sitting in the classroom with the test paper in front of me.)

- for actions which have been repeated frequently over an extended period of time:

   I **have been phoning** you all morning. (It is still morning, and I have phoned you several times.)
   She **has been going** to the same hairdresser for eight years. (Regularly)

- to draw conclusions about past actions from present evidence:

   Someone **has been smoking** in here. (The room smells of smoke.)
   You **have been working out**, haven't you? (You are red and sweating.)

With some _continuity verbs_ (eg, _work, live, wait, sleep_, etc) the present perfect continuous and the present perfect simple are both possible.

   I **have lived/have been living** here for four years.

Otherwise the difference is between an activity which is, or may be, continuing, and an activity which has definitely finished. Compare these two sentences:

a   I **have been mending** the car. (I may, or may not, have finished recently.)
b   I **have mended** the car. (I have definitely finished.)

Stative verbs such as *know, have* (= possess), *believe, like* are seldom used in the continuous form.

I **have known** her all my life. (NOT I *have been knowing her*.)

2   Put the verbs in brackets into the present perfect or the present perfect continuous.

1   This room stinks. Someone _has been smoking_ (smoke) in here.

2   How well can you speak Spanish?

Quite well. I _____ (study) it for the past two years.

3   Where's Margaret?

I don't know. I _____ (not/see) her for ages.

4   You look exhausted. What _____ (you/do)?

I _____ (play) with the kids in the park.

5   _____ (Tim/finish) tidying his room yet?

He _____ (not/start). He _____ (watch) TV all morning.

6   I _____ (try) to get hold of you all afternoon. Where _____ (you/be)?

I _____ (talk) to the boss about the new project.

7   I'm sorry I _____ (not/write) for so long. I _____ (mean) to get in touch for ages, but I _____ (not/have) the time.

8   What is the matter? _____ (you/cry)?

No, it's OK. I _____ (chop) onions.

9   _____ (you/read) Jeffrey's new book yet?

No. I _____ (not/have) the time.

10 Dinner time at last! I _____ (look) forward to this all day.

Me too! I _____ (not/eat) anything since breakfast.

3   Underline the word or phrase which completes the sentence correctly.

1   Deborah *has got/has been getting* ready for the past two hours.

2   I *have had/have been having* a headache since I got out of bed this morning.

3   We have been going to the same doctor *many times/for years*.

4   Your breath smells. *Have you eaten/Have you been eating* garlic?

5   How long *have you known/have you been knowing* Albert?

6   Harry has been making *phone calls/three phone calls* all morning.

7   How many cars *has he sold/has he been selling* this month?

8   We can use the washing machine again now. Gary *has fixed/has been fixing* it.

9   They have been living together *since they left college/on several occasions*.

10 I *have told/have been telling* you for years that you need to do more exercise.

4 Read the text below and look carefully at each line. If the line is correct put a tick (✓). If a line has a word which should not be there, write the word. There are two examples, (0) and (00).

Dear Carlos

0	Thank you for your letter. I'm sorry about I haven't	_about_
00	written for so long, but I've been working very	✓
1	hard recently. My final exams are in the June, you see,	_____
2	and it is very important that I pass them. The reason for	_____
3	I am writing is to ask you if you want to come and	_____
4	stay up with me for a couple of weeks in July. My Uncle	_____
5	Bobby has a farmhouse in Scotland which he lets me	_____
6	to stay in during the summer. The exams will be over by	_____
7	then and I will be really need a break. The farmhouse isn't	_____
8	far from Glasgow, so there I could pick you up from the	_____
9	airport. It will be a very cheap holiday for you because	_____
10	the accommodation it is free, and we will be cooking our	_____
11	own food. Two of my English friends have already agreed	_____
12	to come, so if you will decide that you want to come too, there	_____
13	will be four of us altogether. I really hope so you can make	_____
14	it because I'm sure it's going to be a great fun. Write soon	_____
15	and let me know when you have made a decision yet.	_____

All the best,

Les

Past regrets

Past regrets are expressed with *I wish/if only* + past perfect.

> **I wish I had watched** *that film last night.* (I didn't, and now I wish I had.)
> **If only I had known** *he was a liar.* (I didn't know, and I now regret it.)

We can also use *I regret* + *-ing* form to express regrets in a slightly more formal way.

> *He* **regrets telling** *people about his problem.*
> *I* **regret not working** *harder at school.*

5 Complete the second sentence so that it has a similar meaning to the first sentence. Use the word in bold and other words. Use between two and five words.

1 He wishes he hadn't taken on the job.

taking

He _____ job.

2 I regret lending so much money to Paul.

lent

If _____ so much money to Paul.

3 We are very sorry that we missed your wedding.
wish
We _____ your wedding.

4 I didn't go to university, but now I wish I had.
regret
I _____ to university.

5 Buying this house is something that I really regret doing.
not
If _____ this house.

6 Do you regret not saying goodbye to Anna?
wish
Do _____ goodbye to Anna?

7 She wishes she had worked harder when she was at school.
not
She _____ when she was at school.

8 I really regret not saving any money last year.
had
If _____ money last year.

9 Does he wish he hadn't sold his guitar?
regret
Does _____ his guitar?

10 Bringing the children to see this film was a mistake.
wish
We _____ the children to see this film.

6 Read the text and decide which answer A, B, C or D best fits each space.

Stunt artists

The next time you are watching a film and you see one of the **(0)** _B_ jumping out of a plane, falling off a horse, or being blown through a window - spare a **(1)** ____ for the stunt artist. Lots of people think that stunt artists are just 'extras' who **(2)** ____ small, unimportant parts in films and television. Nothing could be **(3)** ____ from the truth.
A stunt artist must **(4)** ____ the skills of an actor with the physical abilities of a first-**(5)** ____ athlete. He or she must be extremely fit, and **(6)** ____ trained in a number of activities like scuba-diving, horse riding, martial arts or parachuting.
It is not easy to get **(7)** ____ in a career as a stunt performer. Film and television producers look for experience and **(8)** ____ ability, so it is unlikely that they will take on a complete newcomer. However, because of the **(9)** ____ of their profession, stunt artists **(10)** ____ to retire early. This means that new performers must be employed, or there will be no one to take **(11)** ____ when the present generation quits.

Even when a stunt artist becomes well-**(12)** ____, the work is not regular. It may sometimes be necessary to travel to the other side of the world for a job which involves **(13)** ____ hours and great physical danger. It is not a glamorous occupation **(14)** ____ . Unlike the famous actors for **(15)** ____ they sometimes risk their lives, few stunt artists are recognised in the street by adoring fans.

0	**A** personalities	**B** characters	**C** types	**D** identities
1	**A** thought	**B** sympathy	**C** minute	**D** coin
2	**A** make	**B** act	**C** do	**D** play
3	**A** higher	**B** further	**C** nearer	**D** wider
4	**A** mix	**B** consider	**C** consist	**D** combine
5	**A** class	**B** gold	**C** national	**D** level
6	**A** deeply	**B** highly	**C** very	**D** really
7	**A** begun	**B** opened	**C** started	**D** originated
8	**A** shown	**B** proven	**C** definite	**D** doubted
9	**A** nature	**B** kind	**C** way	**D** type
10	**A** lean	**B** rather	**C** bend	**D** tend
11	**A** up	**B** in	**C** over	**D** out
12	**A** famous	**B** heard	**C** spoken	**D** known
13	**A** large	**B** long	**C** big	**D** much
14	**A** too	**B** neither	**C** also	**D** either
15	**A** who	**B** them	**C** whom	**D** which

Third conditional

The third conditional is formed with *if* + past perfect in the conditional clause, and *would* + *have* + past participle in the result clause.

It is used to talk about the imagined consequences of an imaginary past action or situation. For this reason it is sometimes called the *impossible conditional.*

> *If I **hadn't received** an invitation, I **wouldn't have gone** to the party.* (I did receive an invitation, and I did go.)
> *You **would have been arrested if** the police **had caught** you.* (They didn't catch you, so you weren't arrested.)

7 Put the verbs in brackets into the correct form.

1 I'm glad I was sent an invitation to the party. If I <u>hadn't received</u> (not/receive) an invitation, I <u>wouldn't have gone</u> (not/go).

2 Fortunately, Frank was there to help me out of trouble.

You were lucky. What _____ (you/do) if Frank _____ (not/be) there?

3 The ambulance arrived just in time to save her life. She _____ (die) if it _____ (arrive) any later.

4 I washed your shirt by hand. If I _____ (put) it in the machine it _____ (shrink).

5 Why didn't you buy any eggs today?

I _____ (buy) some if I _____ (know) we needed them.

6 How _____ (you/get) home if Terry _____ (not/give) you a lift?

I would have walked, I suppose.

7 Neither of us slept very well last night. I think we _____ (sleep) better if we _____ (not/drink) so much coffee.

8 Ferdinand missed a penalty in the final minute of the match. If he _____ (score), Newcastle _____ (win) the championship.

9 Did you enjoy that film last night?

It was OK, but we _____ (enjoy) it more if the couple behind us _____ (not/talk) all the way through it.

10 Thanks for reminding me about the meeting this evening. I _____ (not/remember) if you _____ (not/say) anything.

8 Complete the second sentence so that it has a similar meaning to the first sentence. Use the word in bold and other words. Use between two and five words.

1 The reason they didn't let you in to the hotel was because you looked so scruffy.

have

They _____ in to the hotel if you hadn't looked so scruffy.

2 Larry was only promoted because he went to the same school as the director.

gone

If Larry _____ to the same school as the director, he wouldn't have been promoted.

3 She didn't ask me to help her, so I didn't.

have

I _____ her if she had asked me.

4 Nobody gave him any encouragement, which is why he didn't succeed.

some

If they _____, he would have succeeded.

5 He didn't tell you because he didn't know.

told

He _____ if he had known.

9 Join the clauses in column A to the clauses in column B to make logical sentences.

A	B
1 If you give me £10	a) we'll arrive at exactly 1.30
2 If I had noticed the door was open	b) we would have found out eventually
3 If you told me you'd seen a ghost	c) I would have fallen asleep
4 If I had had more cash	d) I wouldn't believe you
5 If you leave the key under the mat	e) I wouldn't have to hire a technician
6 If she had told me her life story	f) I would have bought more food
7 Unless my watch is wrong	g) I'll be able to get in without waking anyone
8 If I knew how to repair it	h) I won't tell anyone what you've done
9 If he hadn't told the truth	i) I wouldn't have climbed in through the window

It's a bargain

1 Read the text below and look carefully at each line. If the line is correct put a tick (✓). If a line has a word which should not be there, write the word. There are two examples, (0) and (00).

Supermarkets

0	Nobody can deny that supermarkets are very much	*much*
00	convenient. The whole idea behind them is that they	✓
1	give customers more for choice at a cheaper price. But	_____
2	the current fashion of building enormous supermarkets	_____
3	on the outskirts of towns that is having the opposite effect.	_____
4	These supermarkets are putting off small shopkeepers out	_____
5	of business. Shops in town centres are closing down	_____
6	because they cannot compete up with the low prices the big	_____
7	supermarkets are being able to offer their customers. Town	_____
8	centres are dying. Instead of shopping in town, people	_____
9	are driving them to the out-of-town supermarkets, buying	_____
10	all the food they need for a week or two, then driving	_____
11	home again. That is their choice. But soon they will be have	_____
12	no choice in the matter, because all rest of the shops in their	_____
13	town will have closed down. This is why some of town	_____
14	councils are refusing to give supermarket chains no	_____
15	permission to build in their region. Nobody wants to	_____
	live in a ghost town.	

Modal verbs – obligation

These modal verbs are used to express obligation and prohibition, to give or deny permission and to give advice. Their meanings can be expressed as follows:

Affirmative:	*You **must/have to** do it.*	You are obliged to do it; you have no choice.
	*You **need to** do it.*	It is necessary for you to do it.
	*You **should/ought to** do it.*	You are advised to do it.
	*You **can** do it.*	It is possible/permissible to do it.
	*You **may** do it.*	You have permission to do it.
Negative:	*You **mustn't/can't** do it.*	It is prohibited; you have no choice.
	*You **don't have to/don't need to**.*	It isn't obligatory for you to do it if you don't want to.
	*You **needn't** do it.*	It isn't necessary for you to do it.
	*You **shouldn't** do it.*	You are advised not to do it.

2 Complete the sentences with *must, mustn't or needn't* and one of the verbs below.

open	bring	~~leave~~	make	cook
use	wash	sign	pay	remember

1 If you want to get there on time you *must leave* early in the morning.

2 Tell Judy she _____ tonight. I've ordered a pizza for everyone.

3 I'll give you your birthday present now, but you _____ it until tomorrow.

4 The car isn't very dirty. You _____ it if you don't want to.

5 I promised Hilda I'd be in touch. I _____ to phone her tonight.

6 You _____ a small fee if you want to borrow a CD from the library.

7 Students _____ the computers without first asking permission.

8 We're only going away for two days. Surely you _____ so much luggage with you.

9 All visitors _____ the visitors' book.

10 It's OK, you _____ a decision now. You've got two weeks to think about it.

3 Give advice in these situations using *should(n't)* or *ought to* and the verb in brackets.

1 I've got a really bad cough. – You *shouldn't smoke* so much. (smoke)

2 Robert is getting rather fat. – He _____ on a diet. (go)

3 There is a great film on at the Odeon tonight. – You_____ it. (see)

4 Tom is upset about what they said about his book. – People _____ so much. (criticise)

5 My office is a mess! – You _____ the children play in there. (let)

6 I'm having trouble getting to sleep at night. – You _____ less coffee. (drink)

4 Complete the second sentence so that it has a similar meaning to the first sentence. Use the word in bold and other words. Use between two and five words.

1 A visa is required if you want to visit this country.
   have
   If you want to visit this country, _____ get a visa.

2 The teacher gave us permission to leave the room.
   may
   'You _____, ' the teacher told us.

3 You are obliged to stop when the lights turn red.
   must
   You _____ when the lights turn red.

4 Eating is prohibited in the library.
   must
   You _____ in the library.

5 My accountant advised me not to buy this house.

shouldn't

'You _____,' my accountant said to me.

6 I find it impossible to understand why she refused.

can't

I _____ why she refused.

7 You are not obliged to take part if you don't want to.

needn't

You _____ if you don't want to.

8 Going to school is compulsory until the age of sixteen.

go

Children _____ until they are sixteen.

9 Mum refused us permission to go to the party.

may

'No, _____ to the party,' Mum said.

10 You really should be more careful.

ought

You _____ more careful.

5 Read the text and decide which answer A, B, C or D best fits each space.

Isaac Newton

Sir Isaac Newton, the English scientist and mathematician, was one of the most important figures of the 17th century scientific **(0)** _D_ . One of his greatest **(1)** ____ was the discovery of the three laws of motion, which are still **(2)** ____ today. But he also had a very unusual personality. Some people would **(3)** ____ he was actually insane.

His father died before he was born, and his mother soon remarried. The young Isaac hated his stepfather so much that he once **(4)** ____ to burn his house down - when his stepfather and mother were **(5)** ____ inside! Fortunately he did not, and he **(6)** ____ on to graduate from Cambridge without being thrown into prison.

Isaac's first **(7)** ____ work was a theory of light and colour. When another scientist wrote a paper criticising this theory, Isaac flew into an uncontrollable rage. The scientist **(8)** ____ for the criticism was a man called Robert Hooke. He was head of the Royal Society, and one of the most **(9)** ____ scientists in the country. **(10)** ____, this made no difference to Isaac, who **(11)** ____ to speak to him for over a year.

The **(12)** ____ fact was that Isaac found it impossible to have a calm discussion with anyone. As soon as someone said something that he **(13)** ____ with, he would lose his **(14)** ____ . For this **(15)** ____ he lived a large part of his life isolated from other scientists. It is unlikely that many of them complained.

0	**A** revolt	**B** turning	**C** rise	**D** revolution
1	**A** prizes	**B** achievements	**C** goals	**D** aims
2	**A** forced	**B** used	**C** obeyed	**D** done
3	**A** say	**B** speak	**C** ask	**D** tell
4	**A** shouted	**B** frightened	**C** warned	**D** threatened
5	**A** yet	**B** even	**C** still	**D** now

6	**A** carried	**B** came	**C** went	**D** ran
7	**A** published	**B** released	**C** shown	**D** displayed
8	**A** attributable	**B** reasonable	**C** guilty	**D** responsible
9	**A** regarded	**B** respected	**C** believed	**D** observed
10	**A** However	**B** Although	**C** Despite	**D** What is more
11	**A** supported	**B** denied	**C** ignored	**D** refused
12	**A** easy	**B** simple	**C** straight	**D** honest
13	**A** argued	**B** disliked	**C** disagreed	**D** annoyed
14	**A** temper	**B** mood	**C** character	**D** anger
15	**A** logic	**B** reason	**C** purpose	**D** need

Make, let and *allow*

Make means 'to force' or 'to oblige'. It is followed by the object + infinitive without *to* in active sentences:

> They **made us take** cold showers every morning.

In passive sentences *make* is followed by the *to*-infinitive:

> We **were made to take** cold showers every morning.

Let means 'to permit'. It is only used in the active and is followed by the object + infinitive without *to*:

> My Dad **lets me drive** his car sometimes.

Allow also means 'to permit'. In the active it is followed by the object + *to*-infinitive:

> My Dad **allows me to drive** his car sometimes.

In passive sentences *allow* is followed by the *to*-infinitive:

> I **am allowed to drive** my Dad's car sometimes.

6 Complete the sentences with *make, let* or *allow* in the correct form.

1 They *made* us run five miles every morning. We had no choice.

2 Until what time did your parents _____ you to stay up when you were ten?

3 Do you think it is fair that you are_____ to do military service, even if you think it is wrong?

4 Unfortunately, they won't _____ you leave the country without a passport.

5 _____ me to help you with that suitcase, madam.

6 He can't _____ you do anything you don't want to do.

7 This is an exam. No one is _____ to talk to anyone.

8 If you do not behave yourselves, you will be _____ to stay behind after school.

9 We will not _____ you to go into pubs until you are eighteen.

10 Why do you never _____ me have any fun?

7 Read the text below and think of the word which best fits each space. Use only one word in each space.

The Beatles

The most successful British pop group of **(0)** _all_ time began life as a rock 'n' roll band called 'The Quarrymen' in 1958. They then changed their name **(1)** _____ 'Long John and the Silver Beatles', **(2)** _____ was later shortened to 'The Beatles'. In 1960 and 61 they developed an individual musical style which **(3)** _____ them very popular.

Their first single, *Love me Do,* reached number seventeen **(4)** _____ the pop charts, and in 1963 they had their first number one hit – *From Me to You.* A combination **(5)** _____ charm, humour and excellent pop music contributed **(6)** _____ their incredible popularity, the likes of which had never **(7)** _____ seen before. The nation **(8)** _____ hit by Beatlemania.

John Lennon and Paul McCartney were **(9)** _____ main creative forces behind the group. They composed nearly all of the Beatles' songs, with a few notable exceptions **(10)** _____ as *The Yellow Submarine,* **(11)** _____ Ringo Starr, and George Harrison's *Something.* But by the end of the 60s it was apparent that **(12)** _____ were major artistic differences **(13)** _____ the two, and in 1970 the band broke **(14)** _____.

John Lennon was assassinated in New York in 1980. Fifteen years **(15)** _____ that, the three surviving members reformed and released a single called *Free as a Bird,* which nobody liked.

Wishes

The verb *to wish* can be used in several different ways:

- in set expressions meaning *I hope you have.*

    I **wish** you a **happy birthday/merry Christmas/safe journey,** *etc.*

- with the past perfect to express regrets (see Unit 9 p.65)

- with the past simple to express wishes about states.

    I **wish I lived** in America. (But I do not.)
    I **wish I were** rich. (But I am not.)

- with *could* + infinitive to express wishes about abilities.

    I **wish I could sing**. (But I cannot.)

- with *would* + infinitive to express annoyance at someone or something.

    I **wish you would be** quiet. (You are annoying me with your noise.)
    I **wish it wouldn't rain** so much. (It rains too much, and I don't like it.)

Note: We do not say ~~I wish I would~~ …

---

8 Write sentences with *wish* as in the example.

1 I don't live in America (but I'd like to). I _wish I lived in America_.

2 He lost his keys (and now he is in trouble). He _____.

3 The baby cries all night (and I can't sleep). I _____.

4 She can't drive (but she'd like to). She _____.

5 You're going on a journey (and we hope it's a safe one). We _____.

6 You can smell the pig farm next door (and you don't like it). I _____.

7 I bought an expensive car (and I regret it). I _____.

8 He has to go to hospital (but he doesn't want to). He _____.

9 I'm not very good at maths (but I'd like to be). I _____.

10 You always leave the garage door open (and it annoys me). I _____.

9 Complete the second sentence so that it has a similar meaning to the first sentence. Use the word in bold and other words. Use between two and five words.

1 She would like to be able to speak Italian.
   could
   She _____ Italian.

2 It annoys me that you never do the dishes.
   would
   I _____ the dishes sometimes.

3 I would really like to be famous.
   were
   I _____ famous.

4 We wish you a pleasant flight.
   have
   We hope _____ flight.

5 I would prefer it if I was taller.
   wasn't
   I _____ so short.

6 Does he regret giving her his phone number?
   given
   Does he wish _____ his phone number?

7 He is unhappy because he doesn't have enough money to go on holiday.
   afford
   He _____ to go on holiday.

8 To live on a tropical island would be a dream come true for me.
   lived
   I _____ a tropical island.

9 She is sorry that she didn't bargain with him.
   had
   She _____ with him.

10 A happy new year to you all!
   wish
   I _____ a happy new year!

Our world

1 Read the text below and look carefully at each line. If the line is correct put a tick (✓). If a line has a word which should not be there, write the word. There are two examples, (0) and (00).

Vegetarianism

0	I have many friends who are vegetarians and they	✓
00	often try to convince of me that I should become	*of*
1	one too. They have some very strong arguments in	_____
2	a favour of vegetarianism. Firstly, it is much healthier:	_____
3	vegetarians are less likely than to suffer from	_____
4	heart disease. Secondly, and they say that it is wrong to	_____
5	kill animals just so for food, and it is especially wrong	_____
6	to keep them up in the terrible conditions that most farm	_____
7	animals suffer. I find it very difficult to argue against	_____
8	these points. I have to agree with that it is unhealthy to	_____
9	eat too much of meat, and I hate the cruel way that	_____
10	animals are treated. However, there is one thing that	_____
11	prevents me from becoming a vegetarian: animals are	_____
12	taste *so good*. I would be happily pay extra for meat	_____
13	which comes from animals that have been raised	_____
14	without cruelty. And I don't mind that cutting down on	_____
15	red meat for health reasons. But, for me, life without no	_____
	meat would not be worth living.	

Reported speech

Statements
When reporting statements the tenses usually change in this way:

Direct speech	**Reported speech**
present simple (*'I live'*)	past simple (*He said **he lived***)
present continuous (*'I am living'*)	past continuous (*He said **he was living***)
present perfect (*'I have lived'*)	past perfect (*He said **he had lived***)
present perfect continuous(*'I have been living'*)	past perfect continuous (*He said **he had been living***)
past simple (*'I lived'*)	past perfect (*He said **he had lived***)
past continuous (*'I was living'*)	past perfect continuous (*He said **he had been living***)
going to future (*'I am going to live'*)	*was going to* (*He said **he was going to live***)
will future (*'I will live'*)	*would* (*He said **he would live***)

can ('*I can live*')   *could* (*He said* **he could live**)
may ('*I may live*')   *might* (*He said* **he might live**)
must ('*I must live*')   *had to* (*He said* **he had to live**)

The tenses do not have to change when

- the speaker says something which is always true:

  '*My name is Susan.*' – *She said her name* **is** *Susan.* (It is.)
  '*Toxic gases are dangerous.*' – *She said toxic gases* **are** *dangerous.* (They always are.)

- the time references make it clear when the action happened:

  '*It started to rain when I left the office.*' – *He said that it* **started** *to rain when he* **left** *the office.* (It is clear when both actions happened; the past perfect would only complicate the sentence unnecessarily.)

Time indicators change as follows:

Direct speech	Reported speech
'*today*'	*that day*
'*now*'	*then*
'*here*'	*there*
'*this*'	*that*
'*tonight*'	*that night*
'*tomorrow (night)*'	*the next/following day (night)*
'*next week*'	*the following week*
'*last week*'	*the previous week*
'*yesterday*'	*the previous day*
'*ago*'	*previously/before*

2 Change the following statements into reported speech.

1 'I'm going to Majorca this summer,' he said.

   He <u>said that he was going to Majorca that summer.</u>

2 'Lucy doesn't want to see you tonight,' she told him.

   She _____.

3 'I'm working for Harry this week,' I said.

   I _____.

4 'You must report to the office before you leave,' he told us.

   He _____.

5 'I didn't know about the meeting last week,' I said.

   I _____.

6 'Mark hasn't spoken to his brother for two years,' she said.

   She _____.

7 'By the time we got there all the food had gone,' I said.

   I _____.

8 'I'll phone you if I hear any news,' he told me.

   He _____.

9 'You can stay with me tomorrow, if you want,' she told him.

She _____.

10 'I met Julie about seven years ago,' he said.

He _____.

3   Change the following from reported speech into direct speech.

1 Gary said that he wanted to leave the following day.

Gary said: '_I want to leave tomorrow.'_

2 I told them that they would have to ask permission.

I said: _____.

3 He said we couldn't go out that night.

He said:_____.

4 She told me she had been waiting for hours.

She said:_____.

5 I told him that I had seen her once the previous week.

I said: _____.

6 He said he wasn't going to work that day.

He said: _____.

7 He said that Mary would kill me if she found out.

He said: _____.

8 She said it started to snow when she got up that morning.

She said: _____.

9 I told him that I had left school several years before.

I said: _____.

10 She said that she wouldn't be able to help me until the next day.

She said: _____.

Reported speech

Questions and commands
Questions asked with question words (*who, what, why, where, which, how*) are reported with *asked* + question word. The word order changes back to that of a statement.

> *'What do you want?'- She **asked me what I wanted**.*
> *'Where is the nearest bus stop?' – She **asked where the nearest bus stop was**.*

Questions asked with modal or auxiliary verbs are reported with *asked* + if/whether.

> *'Do you know how to drive, Colin?' – He **asked Colin if/whether he knew how to drive.***

Requests can be reported in two ways:

● using *if*

> *'Will you move over please, Jim?' – He asked Jim **if he would move** over.*

- with a *to* infinitive:

    *He asked Jim **to move** over.*

Commands are reported with an introductory verb like *told, ordered, commanded,* etc + object + *to*-infinitive.

    *'Get out of the house!' – She **told him to get out** of the house.*

---

4 Change the following questions and commands into reported speech.

1 'Did you watch the film on TV last night?' Mary asked me.

Mary *asked me if/whether I had watched the film on TV the previous night*.

2 'Stand up straight!' the sergeant said to him.

The sergeant _____.

3 'When are you going to buy a new car?' he asked me.

He _____.

4 'Will you help me with the baby please, Terry?' she said.

She _____.

5 'Are you aware of the risks involved in the operation?' he asked me.

He _____.

6 'Why have you painted your bedroom walls black?' he asked her.

He _____.

7 'Don't touch the electric fire,' his mother told him.

His mother _____.

8 ' Where is my yellow jumper?' I asked her.

I _____.

9 'Have you heard what Jack did last night?' she asked me.

She _____.

10 'Will you be seeing Jeremy this afternoon?' he asked her.

He _____.

5 Read the text and decide which answer A, B, C or D best fits each space.

Two-Wheelers

The dominant **(0)** _C_ of transport in the twentieth century is undoubtedly the motor car. But as the century draws to a close, a large **(1)** ____ of road users are abandoning these petrol-driven, four-wheeled boxes for a much cleaner, more efficient **(2)** ____ : the bicycle.

It is not a new invention, of course. In 1817, Baron von Drais invented what **(3)** ____ known as the 'running machine'. This was a two-wheeled vehicle which looked very **(4)** ____ to a bicycle, **(5)** ____ that it had no chain or pedals. The rider simply sat in the saddle and ran. It is surprising that these machines were so **(6)** ____ when you consider how uncomfortable they **(7)** ____ have been, but they were very fashionable **(8)** ____ the upper classes.

It was not until 1885 that something truly **(9)** ____ a modern bicycle came onto the market. The 'safety cycle'

(10) ____ the beginning of the age of the two-wheeler. This was not just an expensive (11) ____ for the amusement of the upper classes. It was a cheap and practical machine, and it was not (12) ____ before everyone had one.

With the (13) ____ in car use in the 1950s and 60s, the bicycle went into decline. The car was, after all, faster and more (14) ____ . Until there were so many of them, that is! Nowadays more and more people realise that for city journeys a bicycle can be up to five (15) ____ faster than a car - and it is much easier to find a parking space!

0	**A** way	**B** mark	**C** form	**D** mark
1	**A** number	**B** deal	**C** lot	**D** amount
2	**A** motor	**B** machine	**C** engine	**D** mechanic
3	**A** grew	**B** made	**C** came	**D** became
4	**A** like	**B** same	**C** equal	**D** similar
5	**A** though	**B** yet	**C** except	**D** but
6	**A** usual	**B** general	**C** popular	**D** charming
7	**A** must	**B** can	**C** can't	**D** could
8	**A** around	**B** between	**C** among	**D** inside
9	**A** looking	**B** resembling	**C** appearing	**D** seeming
10	**A** pointed	**B** marked	**C** showed	**D** started
11	**A** joke	**B** play	**C** game	**D** toy
12	**A** far	**B** short	**C** long	**D** ages
13	**A** rise	**B** lift	**C** height	**D** climb
14	**A** easy	**B** soft	**C** comfortable	**D** warmer
15	**A** ways	**B** times	**C** hours	**D** ages

Reporting verbs

Sometimes the meaning of what is said in direct speech can be conveyed in the verb used to report speech.

'I'm sorry for being so late,' he said. - *He **apologised** for being so late.*

These verbs fall into three main types:

- Type A : verb + object + *to* infinitive

    *She **told him to be** quiet.*

Other examples of this type are: *ask, advise, beg, instruct, invite, order, remind, warn.*

- Type B : verb + *to* infinitive

    *I **agreed to help** her.*

Other examples of this type are: *claim, decide, demand, offer, promise, refuse, threaten.*

- Type C : verb + *-ing.*

    *He **denied killing** the policeman.*

Other examples of this type are: *admit, apologise for, regret, suggest.*

6 Change the following sentences into reported speech using one of the verbs below.

invite	offer	suggest	remind	warn
promise	refuse	admit	deny	apologise

1 'I'm sorry that I hurt you,' he said to her.

He _apologised for hurting her_.

2 'I'll give you a lift home if you like,' he said to her.

He _____.

3 'Yes, it was me who crashed into the garage door,' she said.

She _____.

4 'No, I will not lend you a thousand pounds,' she said to him.

She _____.

5 'I will write to you every day,' he said to his mother.

He _____.

6 'Would you like to come to my party?' he said to them.

He _____.

7 'Perhaps going to bed early tonight would be a good idea,' she said.

She _____.

8 'No, I didn't tell anyone about it,' he said.

He _____.

9 'Don't forget to go to the bank, Simon,' she said.

She _____.

10 'Don't eat those mushrooms, or you'll be sick,' she said to him.

She _____.

7 Complete the second sentence so that it has a similar meaning to the first sentence. Use the word in bold and other words. Use between two and five words.

1 'I moved into the flat six months ago,' he said.
   had
   He said that _____ the flat six months before.

2 She denied cheating in the test.
   not
   'I _____ in the test,' she said.

3 'Have you met Samantha?' he asked me.
   whether
   He asked _____ Samantha.

4 'I'm sorry that I didn't recognise you at first' he said to her.

not

He apologised _____ at first.

5 'Where are you going, Thomas?' she said.

was

She _____ going.

6 'Do not try that again,' she said to him.

to

She told _____ that again.

7 'Will you look after my bag for a minute, please?' she asked Ted.

if

She asked _____ look after her bag for a minute.

8 He reminded me to bring my camera.

your

'Don't _____,' he said to me.

9 'Be careful! Those mountains are dangerous,' she said to him.

to

She warned _____, because those mountains are dangerous.

10 Steve invited Sally to the cinema with him.

like

'Would _____ to the cinema with me?' Steve asked Sally.

Impersonal passive

The impersonal passive can be formed in two main ways:

- *It* + passive + *that* clause.
- subject + passive + *to*-infinitive (in all forms).

It is used when there is some doubt about the truth of the statement, or when it is necessary to be cautious and distance the speaker from the statement. Compare these sentences:

a   *Jim tells lies.*
b   ***It is said that*** *Jim tells lies.*
c   ***Jim is said to tell*** *lies.*

Sentence (a) is a direct accusation, and a statement presented as truth. Sentences (b) and (c) are more cautious, and do not involve the speaker in the accusation; the speaker may or may not believe that Jim is a liar.
These verbs are often used in the passive in this way: *believe, consider, know, report, say, suppose, think, understand.*

When the agent is included (for emphasis, or to add important information), it comes after the passive verb.

*He is believed **by the police** to be hiding in Ireland.*

8   Complete the second sentence so that it has a similar meaning to the first sentence. Use the word in bold and other words. Use between two and five words.

1   People say that smoking causes cancer.
    said
    It _____ smoking causes cancer.

2   Nobody believes that Graham was responsible for the fire.
    not
    Graham _____ responsible for the fire.

3   Does anyone consider that the prime minister is an honest man?
    by
    Is the prime minister _____ an honest man?

4   Many people suppose that she is living in Australia.
    be
    She _____ living in Australia.

5   Apparently, nobody has been injured in the explosion.
    reported
    Nobody is _____ in the explosion.

6   People say that Gordon is an excellent swimmer.
    to
    Gordon _____ an excellent swimmer.

7   The police think that the burglar walked in through the front door.
    thought
    It _____ walked in through the front door.

8   We understand that the headmaster is very upset.
    to
    The headmaster _____ very upset.

9   Scientists do not consider this chemical to be dangerous.
    to
    This chemical _____ dangerous.

10 This man is known to be a criminal.
    that
    We _____ a criminal.

9   Use the word at the end of each line to form a word that fits in the space on the same line.

Hunting

In the **(0)** _beginning_, humans hunted because they had to.	**BEGIN**
Until the **(1)** _____ of farming methods, animals had to be	**INTRODUCE**
tracked down and killed in the wild. A **(2)** _____ hunting	**SUCCESS**
trip would **(3)** _____ that the hunters' families did not die of	**SURE**
(4) _____ for another few weeks.	**STARVE**
Nowadays, however, hunting has nothing to do with **(5)** _____.	**SURVIVE**
Fresh meat is easily **(6)** _____ from shops. What is more,	**OBTAIN**
people **(7)** _____ hunt animals which they cannot even eat.	**FREQUENT**
So why do they do it? For some, hunting is a **(8)** _____	**PROFIT**
business. But for others, the only **(9)** _____ seems to be	**EXPLAIN**
that they take some kind of pleasure in **(10)** _____.	**CRUEL**

10   Read the text below and think of the word which best fits each space. Use only one word in each space.

A Bank Robbery

One **(0)** _of_ the simplest cases Inspector Harper **(1)** _____ to solve was a bank robbery which took **(2)** _____ in Leeds in 1968. When he arrived **(3)** _____ the scene of the crime, the cashier explained to him **(4)** _____ had happened.

A tall man in a blue anorak and a motorcycle helmet had walked **(5)** _____ the bank that morning and passed the cashier an envelope **(6)** _____ these words written on the back: 'I HAVE A GUN. HAND OVER ALL THE MONEY AND NO ONE **(7)**_____ GET HURT.' The cashier saw that the man really **(8)** _____ have a gun, and dutifully gave him all the money he had behind the counter. Then the robber put the cash in his bag and ran **(9)** _____ of the door, to the sound of alarm bells.

An hour **(10)** _____the robber was in his house, counting his money, **(11)**_____ Inspector Harper burst through the front door, accompanied **(12)** _____ four large policemen. The poor criminal **(13)** _____ astonished at the speed and efficiency of the West Yorkshire Police. 'How did you know **(14)** _____ was me?' he asked **(15)** _____ amazement. 'Simple, Mr Briggs,' smiled the Inspector. 'Your name and address were written on the front of the envelope!'

Finishing touches

1 Read the text below and think of the word which best fits each space. Use only one word in each space.

The Boss's Hat

I don't usually **(0)** _play_ tricks on people, but when our boss, Mr Budd, bought himself a new hat, my friend **(1)** _____ an idea that was impossible to resist. Every day Mr Budd **(2)** _____ hang up his hat in the hallway and disappear into his office. So one lunch time we went into town and bought two hats identical **(3)** _____ Mr Budd's, except that one was much larger, and the other much smaller, **(4)** _____ his.

When we got **(5)** _____ to the office, we took Mr Budd's hat off the hook and replaced it **(6)** _____ the large one. That evening he **(7)** _____ the hat on and went home, saying nothing to anyone in spite of the **(8)** _____ that his hat was resting on his ears. The next day we substituted the small hat **(9)** _____ the large one, and Mr Budd went home with it sitting high **(10)** _____ top of his head. He looked a bit worried, but he **(11)** _____ didn't say a word to anyone.

This continued for **(12)** _____ few weeks. Sometimes we would put Mr Budd's original hat on the hook, sometimes one **(13)**_____ the others. Everyone in the office knew about the joke, **(14)**_____ Mr Budd. Eventually, he got **(15)** _____ worried that he went to the doctor, convinced that his head was growing and shrinking day by day.

Question tags

Question tags are used in conversation. They are short questions added to statements. A negative statement is followed by an affirmative question tag, and a positive statement is followed by a negative question tag. The auxiliary verb used in the statement is repeated in the question tag or, if there is no auxiliary, the verb *do* is used in the appropriate tense.

Question tags are used to ask for confirmation of, or agreement with, the statement.

> *You don't take sugar, **do you**?* (asking for confirmation)
> *It's freezing today, **isn't it**?* (asking for agreement)

There are a few exceptions to the above rules, including

- imperatives
  *Stop quarrelling, **will you/won't you**?*

- *let's* suggestions
  *Let's make up, **shall we**?*

- *used to*
  *You used to live here, **didn't you**?*

2   Add question tags to the following statements.

1   You don't agree with me, _do you_?

2   Tracy looks well, _____?

3   We used to go to the same school, _____?

4   He couldn't refuse such an offer, _____?

5   You haven't met my sister, _____?

6   Let's go for a drink, _____?

7   Don't forget to post this, _____?

8   We can't go out tonight, _____?

9   Get on with your work, _____?

10   Gary and Phil were very rude, _____?

11   You'll have finished this by next week, _____?

12   He didn't use to have a beard, _____?

13   I'll be safe here, _____?

14   That's not your car, _____?

15   We should come here more often, _____?

3   Read the text and decide which answer A, B, C or D best fits each space.

Krakatoa

A volcanic eruption is possibly the most spectacular **(0)** _A_ of the incredible power of nature - and few eruptions in history have been **(1)** ____ as spectacular as that of Krakatoa. **(2)** ____ the summer of 1883 this volcano, **(3)** ____ on an island between Java and Sumatra, had been quiet for over two hundred years. In May that year came the first **(4)** ____ of renewed activity. Then at 10am on 27 August, the **(5)** ____ island began to explode.

The explosions were heard 3,500 km **(6)** ____ in Australia. Clouds of ash were blown 80 km into the sky, blocking **(7)** ____ the sun and plunging the surrounding areas into complete darkness for two and a half days. This ash **(8)** ____ the Earth several times, causing spectacular red sunsets all over the world **(9)** ____ the following year.

The eruption **(10)** ____ tidal waves which were recorded as far away as South America and Hawaii. The biggest and most **(11)** ____ of these waves was 37m high; it **(12)** ____ out 36,000 people who lived in the coastal towns of Java and Sumatra.

For the next forty-five years the region remained quiet. Then in 1927 a **(13)** ____ of eruptions under the sea led to the **(14)** ____ of a tiny island where Krakatoa once was. This 'Child of Krakatoa' now stands over 200m above sea **(15)** ____ .

0	**A** example	**B** item	**C** exhibit	**D** show
1	**A** quite	**B** just	**C** exactly	**D** really
2	**A** Until	**B** During	**C** When	**D** For
3	**A** living	**B** placed	**C** situated	**D** stationed
4	**A** clues	**B** flags	**C** notices	**D** signs
5	**A** complete	**B** whole	**C** total	**D** full
6	**A** distant	**B** away	**C** long	**D** far

7	**A** over	**B** up	**C** out	**D** on
8	**A** rounded	**B** stretched	**C** circled	**D** surrounded
9	**A** throughout	**B** beyond	**C** without	**D** entire
10	**A** fired	**B** shot	**C** touched	**D** triggered
11	**A** wasteful	**B** destructive	**C** aggressive	**D** constructive
12	**A** cleaned	**B** wiped	**C** poured	**D** dished
13	**A** serial	**B** line	**C** bunch	**D** series
14	**A** appearance	**B** picture	**C** discovery	**D** aspect
15	**A** height	**B** stage	**C** surface	**D** level

Future in the past

The 'future in the past' can be formed with *was/were (just) going to* + infinitive; *was/were about to* + infinitive; *was/were on the point of* + *-ing*; *was/were to* + infinitive; *would* + infinitive.

It is used

- in past narratives to talk about events which were destined to happen.

    *He knew he **was going to be** rich.* (It was his destiny.)
    *They **were to be married** in church later that year.* (It had been arranged.)
    *His four years in prison were nearly over. Soon he **would be** free.*

- to talk about past events which were interrupted.

    *We **were about to leave/on the point of leaving/just going to leave** when the phone rang.*

- to talk about past events which were planned, but did not happen.

    *He **was going to give** me a present, but he left it on the train.*

4 Complete the sentences with one of the phrases below, in the correct form. You will have to use each phrase more than once. Sometimes more than one answer is possible.

would be	be on the point of	be to
be going to	be about to	

1 He *was on the point of* going home, when he received an urgent message.

2 They could see the lights of the town in the distance. Soon they _____ warm and safe in their own home.

3 Nobody could have known that Matthew _____ be so rich and famous when he grew up.

4 I was surprised at how angry Sophie was when I told her the news. I thought she _____ pleased.

5 I noticed there was a cat sleeping under the wheels of the car just as Mark _____ start the engine and drive off.

6 The mountaineers _____ giving up all hope of rescue, when a helicopter appeared over the hill.

7 I'm sorry. I _____ cook you a meal, but I didn't have time to go to the supermarket.

8 It was all arranged. I _____ drive to London, pick up the package, and deliver it to Jenkins by 6 o'clock that evening.

9 When she was a girl she always said that she _____ buy a house in France, but she has never left England - not even for a holiday.

10 Our weekend had been carefully planned. We _____ catch the five o'clock train to Bradford, where we _____ met by Aunt Miriam.

5 Read the text below and look carefully at each line. If the line is correct put a tick (✓). If a line has a word which should not be there, write the word. There are two examples, (0) and (00).

Dear Les

0	Thank you for inviting me to come and spend the	✓
00	summer with you in Scotland. It sounds like absolutely	*like*
1	wonderful. Unfortunately not, it is impossible for me to	_____
2	accept your invitation as I have already arranged to	_____
3	spend the summer with my cousins there in America. If	_____
4	only that you had written a month earlier, I would not have	_____
5	hesitated to accept your offer. To be honest, I would	_____
6	much prefer it to spend the holidays with you than with	_____
7	my cousins who, I am sorry to say, they are rather boring.	_____
8	But never mind - maybe I could find out some time to	_____
9	come and see you later in the year. Or maybe you could	_____
10	come and visit me. There is a quite spare room in our house,	_____
11	and my parents would be such happy to see you. Do you	_____
12	remember the last time you were here? What a fun we had!	_____
13	If you do decide to visit, it will have to be some time after	_____
14	July, as I am in America until then time. Please write back	_____
15	soon and tell to me what you have decided. Give my love	_____

to your Mum and Dad.

Best wishes

Carlos

Do

Apart from the obvious uses of *do* to form questions and negatives, it can be used to add emphasis to a verb, or to act as a substitute for a longer phrase to avoid repetition.

> *I **do** like contemporary art.* (Emphasis – I think it's great; or – you said I didn't like it, and I am contradicting you.)
> *He doesn't want to go, but she **does**.* (Substitute for the longer phrase, *wants to go*.)

It can also be used with imperatives to add emphasis.

> ***Do** come to the party.* (I would really like it if you did.)

6 Read the situations and write what you would say in each of them, using *do* in the correct form.

1 Your friend thinks you don't like pop music. This is not true.

You say: 'I *do like pop music.* '

2 Tom wants you to go to a horror film with him. You hate horror films. He can't understand why.

You say: 'You may enjoy seeing violence and blood at the cinema, but _____.'

3 The children are being very noisy. You would really like them to be quiet.

You say: '_____.'

4 You know that Gordon wants to play in the team. Your friend does not believe you.

You say: 'Gordon _____.'

5 Sally likes sailing. Fred hates it. Your friend wants to invite them both to go sailing with him. You tell him it's a bad idea, and he wants to know why.

You say: 'Because Sally _____, _____.'

6 Your mother accuses Tim of not working hard at school. You know this is not fair.

You say: 'Tim _____.'

7 You see your friend's new baby boy. You think he looks very much like his father.

You say: 'He _____.'

8 Someone tells you that a colleague of yours didn't go to university. You know this is not true.

You say: 'She _____.'

9 Harry is a vegetarian. John is not. Your friend wants to know why you invited John to the barbecue, but not Harry.

You say: 'Because Harry doesn't _____, _____.'

10 Your Mum and Dad are flying to Bangkok. You are worried about the long flight, and would really like them to phone you as soon as they arrive.

You say: '_____.'

Multi-word verbs

7 Use the correct form of the verbs below to rewrite the second sentence so that it means exactly the same as the first sentence.

break out	sort out	take to	get by
drop off	wipe out	turn up	catch up with

1 It is said that the Ice Age **destroyed** the dinosaurs.

It is said that the dinosaurs _____.

2 It was several weeks before he **started to like** his new surroundings.

It was several weeks _____.

3 Any further problems will be **dealt with** by my lawyer.

My lawyer _____.

4 **Fewer** people are buying digital watches **than before**.

The number of people buying _____.

5 The police **found** the kidnappers as they were trying to leave the country.

The police _____.

6 If it wasn't for mother's part-time job, I don't think we could **manage**.

I don't think _____.

7 The fire **started** on the fifth floor of the building.

The fire_____.

8 Tony finally **got here** at midnight.

Tony _____.

Final Tests

Test 1

1 Read the text and decide which answer A, B, C or D best fits each space.

Acupuncture

Acupuncture is a Chinese method of **(0)** _D_ illnesses by inserting needles into certain points of the body. The idea is that this restores the natural **(1)** ____ of energy, which is disturbed when a person is ill. The origins of this therapy have been traced **(2)** ____ over five thousand years, but it only began to be **(3)** ____ in the West in the 1970s.

In 1971, James Reston, a well-**(4)** ____ journalist from the *New York Times*, was visiting China when he developed appendicitis. He was operated **(5)** ____ in a hospital in Peking, where the doctors used acupuncture to **(6)** ____ his pain. Reston was surprised at how **(7)** ____ it was, and wrote about it in an article for the newspaper.

Soon afterwards, Chairman Mao Tse-tung invited a group of **(8)** ____ Western doctors over to China to witness for themselves that acupuncture **(9)** ____ . They were accompanied **(10)** ____ television crews, and soon viewers in the West were watching operations being **(11)** ____ out on patients with acupuncture needles sticking out of them. The patients felt **(12)** ____ pain.

The Western experts were a **(13)** ____ embarrassed at what they saw, because they had **(14)** ____ ridiculed the idea that patients could be treated with needles. But now they were **(15)** ____ to admit that it actually worked, and acupuncture became a popular form of therapy.

0	**A** improving	**B** doctoring	**C** practising	**D** treating
1	**A** scale	**B** balance	**C** mirror	**D** weight
2	**A** back	**B** forward	**C** up	**D** towards
3	**A** admitted	**B** accepted	**C** taken	**D** held
4	**A** famous	**B** heard	**C** celebrated	**D** known
5	**A** at	**B** over	**C** in	**D** on
6	**A** release	**B** repair	**C** relieve	**D** retain
7	**A** influential	**B** effective	**C** practical	**D** used
8	**A** distinguished	**B** impressive	**C** distinct	**D** related
9	**A** did	**B** worked	**C** won	**D** made
10	**A** to	**B** with	**C** by	**D** of
11	**A** acted	**B** brought	**C** performed	**D** carried
12	**A** not	**B** any	**C** no	**D** none
13	**A** little	**B** tiny	**C** quite	**D** rather
14	**A** early	**B** before	**C** previously	**D** anciently
15	**A** had	**B** forced	**C** pushed	**D** strengthened

2 Read the text below and think of the word which best fits each space. Use only one word in each space.

A True Story

My friend Colin is a very keen golfer. We play together every Sunday, but I seldom win because he is **(0)** *much* better than me. I suspect that **(16)** ____ of the reasons why he came to be **(17)** ____ a good player is that, **(18)** ____ many top sportsmen, he hates losing. Let me give you an example.

One Sunday, we were playing **(19)** ____ other in the club championship. There were quite a **(20)** ____ people watching. Colin started badly, and I won the first two holes, but I expected **(21)** ____ he would soon catch up and beat me. He didn't. Every shot he made went off to one side, into the woods or into a bunker. I **(22)** ____ see that Colin was getting increasingly angry.

On the eighteenth hole, Colin's first shot landed **(23)** ____ the pond. With a cry **(24)** ____ despair he picked up his golf bag, swung it around **(25)** ____ head and threw it **(26)** ____ the middle of the pond. Then he stormed off past the clubhouse to his car. A few seconds **(27)** ____, we heard another cry, and saw Colin walk **(28)** ____ in our direction. As he passed me he said "This is not a good day for me", and carried **(29)** ____ walking into the water. When he reached the middle of the pond, he felt around under the surface and lifted out his golf bag. Then he put his hand into the bag, and pulled **(30)** ____ his soaking wet car keys.

3 Complete the second sentence so that it has a similar meaning to the first sentence. Use the word in bold and other words. Use between two and five words.

31 My hair really needs to be cut soon.

must

I really _____ cut soon.

32 It is much too cold to go to the beach today.

warm

It _____ to go to the beach today.

33 I regret not accepting the job.

wish

I _____ the job.

34 She thought that the police were following her.

followed

She thought that _____ by the police.

35 You might get hungry, so I put some sandwiches in your bag.

case

I put some sandwiches in your bag _____ hungry.

36 Perhaps Tracy had to go home.

might

Tracy _____ to go home.

37 Will you take care of the dog while I'm on holiday?

after

Will you _____ while I'm on holiday?

38   'I'm sorry that I didn't write to you, Anna,' said Gerry.
      apologised
      Gerry _____ to Anna.

39   Could you hold this for a moment, please?
      mind
      Would _____ for a moment, please?

40   The authorities didn't give me permission to visit the prisoner.
      allow
      The authorities didn't _____ the prisoner.

4   Read the text below and look carefully at each line. If the line is correct put a tick (✓). If a line has a word
      which should not be there, write the word. There are two examples, (0) and (00).

Health and Fitness

0	It is important in today's society to keep as fit and	✓
00	healthy as possible. People who do work in offices have	*do*
41	to be especially sure that they take over some form of	_____
42	exercise at least twice a week if they want to live for	_____
43	a long and happy life. But what is it the best way to	_____
44	keep fit? It really depends on your personality. If you	_____
45	are a competitive kind of person, then you would have	_____
46	probably like to play with some kind of sport. The kind of	_____
47	sport would, again, depend on you. A sociable type	_____
48	would prefer to team sports, whereas a 'loner' would	_____
49	be attracted to individual sports like tennis, squash or	_____
50	badminton. For those who they do not want to compete, there	_____
51	are many of alternatives to sport. Walking, cycling and	_____
52	running are all the cheap and enjoyable forms of exercise.	_____
53	There are also many gymnasiums and health clubs to	_____
54	join up, which provide weight training facilities, and	_____
55	sometimes offer a personal training to suit your individual	_____
	needs.	

5 Use the word at the end of each line to form a word that fits in the space on the same line.

Driven Crazy

Every car driver knows how **(0)** _frustrating_ it can be to be stuck   FRUSTRATE
in a traffic jam. The **(56)** _____ becomes unbearable at times, and   BORE
can **(57)** _____ lead to aggression, or even violence against other   OCCASION
drivers. Such **(58)** _____ is becoming more and more common these   BEHAVE
days. So common, in fact, that **(59)** _____ have come up with a   PSYCHOLOGY
name for it: 'road rage'.

It is not just traffic jams which can cause an otherwise **(60)** _____ and   PEACE
law-abiding citizen to change into a dangerous and **(61)** _____ monster.   ABUSE
Many things can **(62)** _____ him: another driver stealing a parking   RAGE
space, for example, or someone **(63)** _____ in the wrong lane   TAKE
of a motorway. Anything, in fact, which could be seen as an **(64)** _____   INVADE
of **(65)** _____ territory. It seems that man's primitive instincts are   PERSON
awakened when he gets behind a steering-wheel.

Test 2

1 Read the text and decide which answer A, B, C or D best fits each space.

Spelling

Spelling **(0)** _D_ a major problem to many students – and, indeed, native speakers – of English. This is
(1) ____ surprising when you consider just how illogical the English spelling **(2)** ____ is. The spelling of such
basic words as _right, through, once,_ and _who_ seems to **(3)** ____ no relation to their **(4)** ____ . And how can the
words _go, sew,_ and _though_ all rhyme with **(5)** ____ other?
There have been attempts in the **(6)** ____ to reform English spelling. The playwright George Bernard Shaw
was an enthusiastic **(7)** ____ for a more phonetic approach. In a clever illustration of the absurdity of English
spelling he suggested that the word _fish_ be **(8)** ____ by the letters 'ghoti': the _gh_ from _enough,_ the _o_ from
women, and the _ti_ from _nation._ When he died in 1950 he **(9)** ____ a large part of his estate to promote spelling
reform.
So why do we **(10)** ____ in spelling words the way we do, **(11)** ____ the efforts of reformers like Shaw? One
reason is that we are too **(12)** ____ with the words as they are currently spelled. It is certain that any change in
the rules **(13)** ____ be extremely difficult, if not impossible, to **(14)** ____ . Another is that there is **(15)** ____ a
variety of regional accents within the English speaking world that it would be unfair to select just one as the
standard model for spelling.

0	**A** makes	**B** puts	**C** shows	**D** presents
1	**A** just	**B** hardly	**C** nearly	**D** strongly
2	**A** system	**B** procedure	**C** method	**D** schedule
3	**A** hold	**B** keep	**C** carry	**D** bear
4	**A** voice	**B** speech	**C** vocation	**D** pronunciation
5	**A** the	**B** every	**C** each	**D** one
6	**A** history	**B** years	**C** past	**D** ages
7	**A** campaigner	**B** demonstrator	**C** champion	**D** candidate
8	**A** described	**B** represented	**C** signed	**D** written

9   **A** willed   **B** left   **C** gave   **D** divided
10 **A** insist   **B** continue   **C** keep   **D** persist
11 **A** in spite   **B** despite   **C** however   **D** although
12 **A** accustomed **B** used   **C** friendly **D** familiar
13 **A** would   **B** could   **C** ought   **D** should
14 **A** require   **B** enforce   **C** make   **D** oblige
15 **A** many   **B** quite   **C** such   **D** so

2 Read the text below and think of the word which best fits each space. Use only one word in each space.

Bee Keeping

Honey, the sweetest **(0)** _of_ natural foods, was the main source of sugar in ancient times. It was highly prized both as a foodstuff **(16)** _____ a medicine. In those days, the art of bee keeping was known only **(17)** _____ a select few members of secret societies, who were treated **(18)** _____ great respect. Nowadays, of course, bee-keeping is not surrounded by such mystique. It is a popular pastime **(19)** _____ can be taken up by anyone with a **(20)** _____ money to spend and some space in their garden.

It **(21)** _____ be wrong to say that bees are domestic creatures, farmed **(22)** _____ the same way as cows or sheep. The beekeeper provides a home for the bees, and **(23)** _____ care of them, but the bees remain wild. In a sense, the relationship **(24)** _____ bee and beekeeper is one of mutual exploitation. Both benefit **(25)** _____ the relationship, and neither one is a slave to the other.

Many people **(26)** _____ an irrational fear of bees. Their anxiety is usually based **(27)**_____ an ignorance of **(28)** _____ true nature of these adorable insects. They are not naturally aggressive creatures. True, their sting is rather painful, but it is seldom **(29)** _____ serious for the victim as it is for the bee, who dies soon **(30)** _____.

3 Complete the second sentence so that it has a similar meaning to the first sentence. Use the word in bold and other words. Use between two and five words.

31 Can you tell me who this car belongs to?
    car
    Can you tell me _____ is?

32 I heard a scream just as I was about to fall asleep.
    point
    I was _____ asleep when I heard a scream.

33 He wishes he had saved some money.
    regrets
    He _____ any money.

34 Somebody has to collect the kids from school.
    picked
    The children _____ from school.

35 'What have you done with the car keys, Katie?' asked John.
    she
    John asked Katie _____ with the car keys.

36 Without your encouragement, we would not have won.
    you
    We would not have won _____ us.

37 Her voice was so quiet that we could hardly hear her.
    such
    She _____ that we could hardly hear her.

38 Going to parties was not something we did very often.
    use
    We _____ to parties very often.

39 Running is not allowed in the corridors.
    must
    You _____ in the corridors.

40 It is not possible that Jenkins took the money.
    have
    Jenkins _____ the money.

4 Read the text below and look carefully at each line. If the line is correct put a tick (✓). If a line has a word which should not be there, write the word. There are two examples, (0) and (00).

A Restaurant

0	*The Pot* is one of the nicest restaurants in this area.	✓
00	It is situated in a little back street near from the central	*from*
41	square, so a visitor to the town could be easily miss it	_____
42	if he or she were not actually looking for it. It is always	_____
43	busy in the evenings, so that it is essential to book a table	_____
44	before you go, in order to avoid the disappointment. When	_____
45	you arrive a waiter he will show you to your table, hand you	_____
46	the menu and ask about if you want anything to drink. There	_____
47	is a fantastic selection of good wines to choose from. The	_____
48	décor is simple but tasteful, with a few of modern paintings	_____
49	on the walls, and flowers and candles on every table.	_____
50	Classical music is being played quietly in the background. But	_____
51	the best thing about *The Pot* is definitely the food. Every	_____
52	night you can to choose from only four or five different	_____
53	dishes, but they are all so expertly prepared that the	_____
54	lack of choice it does not matter. They are all absolutely	_____
55	delicious. The only bad thing I have to say you about *The Pot*	_____
	is that it is quite expensive, and I cannot afford to go there every day!	_____

5 Use the word at the end of each line to form a word that fits in the space on the same line.

The National Lottery

The National Lottery has come in for a lot of **(0)** _criticism_	**CRITIC**
since its **(56)** _____ in 1995. A proportion of the profits	**INTRODUCE**
was supposed to go towards **(57)** _____ charities and	**VARY**
(58) _____ institutions; but charities seem to be worse off	**CULTURE**
than before. The reason for this is that lottery **(59)** _____	**PLAY**
are less **(60)** _____ to give money to charity, because they	**WILL**
believe that by buying a ticket they are **(61)** _____	**EFFECT**
making a donation **(62)** _____.	**ANY**
(63) _____, the charities and institutions which benefit	**FURTHER**
from lottery money are often thought to be **(64)** _____	**DESERVE**
by the general public. The most **(65)** _____ example of this	**FAME**

is the Royal Opera House. Is its need greater than, for example,
that of the Cancer Research Fund?

Answer key

Unit 1

Exercise 1
0 D	6 D	11 A
2 D	7 C	12 B
3 A	8 D	13 A
4 B	9 C	14 D
5 A	10 C	15 C

Exercise 2
2 is sunbathing
3 Are you watching
4 do not speak
5 is looking
6 usually finishes
7 Do you know, I'm learning
8 is Joe going, always carries
9 think, is sleeping
10 do not like, love

Exercise 3
2 a wears	b am wearing
3 a am doing	b do
4 a are having	b has
5 a is making	b makes
6 a do you think	b is thinking

Exercise 4
2 are you crying
3 when
4 are working
5 because Mum told
6 every day
7 when he can afford it
8 are you cooking
9 temporarily
10 fall

Exercise 5
1 ✓
2 much
3 so
4 to
5 are
6 ✓
7 no
8 of
9 out
10 ✓
11 with
12 making
13 ✓
14 the
15 about

Exercise 6
2 A beautiful old wooden desk.
3 Some blue plastic flowers.
4 A funny old American film.
5 A huge concrete building.
6 An expensive red Italian racing car.
7 A comfortable big leather sofa.
8 An ugly pear-shaped glass vase.
9 Some horrible little brown insects.
10 A mysterious triangular metal object.

Exercise 7
2 big old Japanese
3 beige plastic
4 fashionable long-sleeved silk
5 pessimistic young

Exercise 8
1 have	6 who	11 so
2 at	7 like	12 the
3 time	8 both	13 in
4 as	9 which	14 that
5 was	10 of	15 by

Exercise 9
2 in case he meets any dangerous animals.
3 He's taking medicine in case he becomes ill.
4 He's taking a map in case he gets lost.
5 He's taking some presents in case he meets any friendly locals.
6 He's taking a mobile phone in case he needs to call for help.

Exercise 10
2 because Tom might/may
3 in case we ran out
4 in case you should
5 in case nobody speaks
6 because you might want
7 in case we wanted
8 in case we do not
9 because you might want
10 in case she forgot

Exercise 11
1 professional	6 Unfortunately
2 decision	7 employers
3 knowledge	8 idealistic
4 wealthy	9 surprising
5 satisfaction	10 impatient

Unit 2

Exercise 1
1 so	6 ✓	11 that
2 are	7 the	12 when
3 ✓	8 as	13 ✓
4 had	9 ✓	14 up
5 they	10 much	15 ✓

Exercise 2
2 get used to queuing
3 'm not used to (eating) spicy food
4 getting used to (using) word processors
5 got used to flying
6 are used to the heat/have got used to the heat
7 get used to the noise
8 was not used to (eating in) expensive restaurants
9 wasn't used to obeying orders
10 getting used to horses

Exercise 3
1 was getting used to
2 am not used to sleeping
3 will get used to milking
4 am used to
5 get used to being
6 was not used to riding
7 am not used to
8 was getting used to (driving)
9 got used to being/life as
10 am used to receiving

Exercise 4
1 C	6 B	11 B
2 A	7 A	12 B
3 D	8 C	13 D
4 D	9 A	14 C
5 B	10 D	15 C

Exercise 5
2 have you done, put
3 saw, has not changed
4 passed, got
5 has not been, won
6 have never eaten, have eaten
7 have you been, went, haven't been
8 did Paul and Sue get, didn't go
9 has left, wasn't, haven't been
10 have just read, did you spend
11 have looked, haven't found, Have you tried, had
12 haven't seen, didn't recognise, 've lost
13 've worked, didn't give, asked, has never liked
14 learned, never had to, met, have learned
15 've broken, did you do, tried

Exercise 6
2 Did you lose
3 yet
4 didn't snow
5 a thousand times
6 Have you washed
7 in
8 this
9 have never been
10 haven't heard

Exercise 7

1 of	6 same	11 most
2 was	7 taken	12 is
3 That	8 for	13 which/that
4 with	9 from	14 up
5 so	10 there	15 leave

Exercise 8

2 worse
3 further
4 easier
5 better
6 more expensive
7 more carefully
8 sunnier
9 more patient
10 louder

Exercise 9

1 never be the same weight
2 not as rich as
3 are more intelligent than
4 Beckett writes as well as
5 is just as expensive as
6 further than he
7 the same height as
8 worse than I
9 behave as well as
10 are safer drivers than

Exercise 10

2 it has gone off
3 gave up his job in order to go back to university
4 has always dreamt of setting up her own business
5 wore off as time went on
6 got on (well) with his boss
7 was brought up
8 have worn out
9 is very good at sorting out other people's problems
10 Grow up

Unit 3

Exercise 1

2 are having our bungalow modernised
3 you have your clothes designed
4 not have my homework checked
5 have to get
6 always had her breakfast made
7 is teaching my son
8 to have your appendix
9 get this report translated
10 loves having its head

Exercise 2

2 had/got it translated
3 do you have/get your eyes tested
4 didn't you have/get this film developed
5 have/get my nose pierced
6 have had/got it trained
7 are having/getting a new bathroom fitted
8 have had it dyed
9 Have you had it serviced
10 do not have/get new computers installed

Exercise 3

1 loneliness	6 outside	
2 employment	7 technological	
3 surrounded	8 spoken	
4 rarely	9 warmth	
5 communication	10 digital	

Exercise 4

2 had/got his driving licence taken away by the police
3 had/got his nose broken in a car crash
4 will have/get all your money stolen if you go into that park at night
5 had/got my face scratched when I was playing with the cat

Exercise 5

2 need feeding
3 needs tidying
4 need disciplining
5 needs repairing
6 needs cutting
7 needs servicing

Exercise 6

1 with	6 with	11 was
2 that	7 have	12 from
3 are	8 gave	13 tell
4 find	9 back	14 to
5 been	10 would/might	15 on

Exercise 7

2 someone else's bag
3 Terry and Judy's farm
4 anybody's seat?
5 in other people's problems
6 are someone else's toys
7 to John and Paula's wedding?
8 my parents' building

Exercise 8

1 since	6 much	11 for
2 for	7 the	12 be
3 they	8 ✓	13 out
4 ✓	9 of	14 ✓
5 she	10 ✓	15 about

Exercise 9

2 she was a little girl
3 wrote
4 they closed it down
5 for
6 months
7 for
8 this morning
9 for five years
10 for

Exercise 10

2 ages since she spoke
3 had my car serviced since
4 has been crying since
5 have been married for
6 have not been sailing for
7 living in this city for
8 been training every day since
9 not seen her parents since
10 ages since you bought

Exercise 11

1 A	6 D	11 C
2 B	7 A	12 B
3 C	8 D	13 A
4 B	9 B	14 D
5 D	10 B	15 C

Unit 4

Exercise 1

1 it	6 their	11 the
2 been	7 about	12 had
3 lot	8 ✓	13 of
4 ✓	9 to	14 ✓
5 out	10 ✓	15 us

Exercise 2

2 were you doing
3 jumped, rescued
4 saw, was living
5 did you go, got off
6 rang, were playing
7 wrote
8 was writing, walked
9 Were you working, went
10 were sleeping, got
11 did that newsreader say, wasn't listening
12 took, was having
13 Did you see, was trying
14 didn't know, broke down
15 was raining, were crying, decided

Exercise 3

3 I'm afraid I didn't hear what you said
4 Alan was reading a newspaper when he heard a strange noise
5 She knew she was being followed
6 The boss walked in while I was playing a computer game
7 ✓
8 He read the entire book, from start to finish, in two hours
9 ✓
10 I didn't see the last goal because I was looking at the sky at the time

Exercise 4

1 might have given her
2 can't have known
3 may not have wanted
4 could have forgotten

5 must have been telling
6 he has already seen
7 can't have been
8 must have been driving
9 might have been
10 may not have received

Exercise 5
2 can't
3 must
4 could
5 can't
6 must
7 may
8 must
9 can't
10 must

Exercise 6
1 is	6 to	11 has/had
2 and	7 who	12 such
3 at	8 invite	13 which/that
4 for	9 will	14 Nobody
5 get	10 one	15 with

Exercise 7
2 where
3 whose
4 ——
5 when
6 ——
7 which/that
8 who
9 ——
10 which/that

Exercise 8
1 a friend who owns
2 is the room which
3 a cat that just sleeps
4 reason why he is
5 was (the year) when
6 the girl whose calculator
7 the man whom they interviewed
8 two brothers who are (both)
9 the roof of which
10 the town where

Exercise 9
1 B	6 D	11 A
2 A	7 B	12 C
3 D	8 B	13 D
4 D	9 C	14 D
5 B	10 B	15 B

Exercise 10
2 did you decide to call off the match/call the match off
3 picks him up from school
4 some time to work out this problem/work this problem out
5 takes up a lot of her time
7 went through my homework before I handed it in

7 who carried out this terrible crime
8 dropped out of the course because he found a job in marketing
9 put me off entering the building
10 can settle up at the end of the month

Unit 5

Exercise 1
1 far
2 able
3 to
4 this/that
5 without
6 had
7 until
8 was
9 it
10 for
11 been
12 made
13 as
14 in
15 next/following

Exercise 2
1 used to take her
2 I would go
3 do not usually spend
4 did not use to listen
5 used to crash his bike
6 don't/do not usually lend money
7 would play badminton
8 you use to visit
9 did not use to go
10 would never take a map

Exercise 3
2 used to drink
3 used to hate
4 used to
5 Did you use to live
6 is usually
7 we used to go/would go
8 used to be
9 didn't/did not use to speak/talk
10 doesn't/does not usually wear

Exercise 4
1 competition
2 dangerous
3 regulations
4 unfairly
5 Professional
6 adventurous
7 understanding
8 safety
9 knowingly
10 achievement

Exercise 5
2 realised, had lost
3 lost, had never played
4 had bought, tried

5 was, had visited
6 dropped, burst
7 didn't you speak, had left
8 you didn't eat, couldn't help, had just eaten
9 looked, hadn't seen
10 took, got, refused, had forgotten
11 had spent, realised, had done, had robbed, had burgled, had stolen, had never killed

Exercise 6
1 had never been on television
2 had gone/left by the
3 had never met him
4 before they signed
5 had never stayed
6 had just finished
7 he had written
8 she (had) turned off
9 we arrived soon
10 after I had checked

Exercise 7   Exercise 8
Exercise 7	Exercise 8
1 D	1 too
2 A	2 ✓
3 C	3 having
4 D	4 are
5 B	5 ✓
6 C	6 they
7 A	7 our
8 D	8 out
9 B	9 the
10 A	10 ✓
11 D	11 made
12 B	12 them
13 A	13 ✓
14 C	14 so
15 D	15 ✓

Unit 6

Exercise 1
2 scruffily-dressed man
3 image-conscious
4 five-minute walk
5 cleverly-planned attack
6 short-legged cat
7 angry-looking woman
8 four-year degree course
9 horrible-smelling perfume
10 card-carrying members

Exercise 2
1 B	6 D	11 C
2 A	7 B	12 D
3 A	8 A	13 D
4 C	9 A	14 A
5 C	10 C	15 A

Exercise 3
2 by	5 on	8 by
3 in	6 on	9 in
4 on	7 by	10 by

Exercise 4
1 by plane/on a plane
2 is on the
3 work on foot
4 travelling by bicycle
5 drove to Wales in

Exercise 5
1 ✓	6 that	11 self
2 the	7 ✓	12 ✓
3 of	8 this	13 and
4 being	9 have	14 ✓
5 ✓	10 ✓	15 so

Exercise 6
2 are going to miss
3 am not working
4 doesn't start
5 am going
6 are going to faint
7 isn't going to like
8 am cooking
9 is going to look
10 don't close

Exercise 7
1 he is going to join
2 he is going to have
3 leaves/departs at
4 am meeting my bank manager
5 it is going to
6 are you going to do
7 is never going to drink
8 are not doing
9 am not going to help
10 does not begin

Exercise 8
2 such a	5 so	8 so
3 so	6 such a	9 such
4 such	7 so	10 so

Exercise 9
1 was so little food
2 is such a good writer
3 has got such strong
4 is so confident
5 such a large number
6 was so happy
7 the piano so badly
8 have (got) so much money
9 was so angry
10 much to do - so little

Exercise 10
1 as	6 known	11 a
2 not	7 one	12 for
3 be	8 was	13 since
4 the	9 with	14 all
5 it	10 of	15 search

Exercise 11
1 set off for France on 1 April
2 checked out (of the hotel) this morning

---

3 supply of food is running out/has almost run out
4 caught a lot of people out/caught out a lot of people
5 never really took off in the United States
6 call on me when you were in town
7 calls for a great deal of strength and fitness
8 take part in the fighting at the football match

Unit 7

Exercise 1
2 to finish
3 hitting
4 speaking/to speak
5 to care
6 skiing, falling
7 dining, to eat
8 to lend, losing
9 to do/doing, joining
10 to help, getting

Exercise 2
1 it	6 for	11 not
2 like	7 ✓	12 will
3 in	8 a	13 ✓
4 of	9 to	14 side
5 ✓	10 ✓	15 been

Exercise 3
1 shouting	6 to inform
2 to lock	7 to get
3 to phone	8 giving
4 making	9 crying, feeding
5 to go	10 to close, putting

Exercise 4
1 you keep making
2 I felt like going
3 regret spending
4 not resist telling her
5 will never forget meeting
6 denied shooting
7 you mind opening the window
8 did not seem to be
9 you offer to help
10 could not help laughing

Exercise 5
1 A	6 A	11 D
2 D	7 D	12 C
3 B	8 B	13 B
4 C	9 C	14 C
5 B	10 A	15 A

Exercise 6
2 too cold
3 fit enough
4 enough people
5 too much

---

6 clever enough
7 enough money
8 enough room, too many
9 too young, enough qualifications
10 well enough, too hard

Exercise 7
1 will buy
2 get
3 will meet
4 fall
5 comes
6 apologise
7 dies
8 won't come
9 'll sell
10 Will you give
11 break
12 learns
13 'll take
14 starts, stops

Exercise 8
2 will be
3 I'll give
4 is meeting
5 am not going to speak
6 does
7 won't get
8 I'll just go
9 She's working
10 I'll bring

Exercise 9
1 come
2 who
3 on
4 between
5 it
6 could
7 either
8 that
9 his
10 from
11 would
12 where
13 until
14 off
15 have

Exercise 10
2 The building which I'm working in has no heating.(no commas)
3 Mrs Phillips, whose daughter is an actress, owns five televisions. (2 commas)
4 Only a few people who play the lottery actually win anything. (no commas)
5 World War 1, which lasted four years, was fought mainly in Europe. (2 commas)
6 The man who lives downstairs from me likes heavy metal music. (no commas)
7 Steven lives in a town which has very few restaurants.(no commas)

8 We are going to spend a week in Prague, where our friends live.(1 comma)

9 Do you remember the time when we got lost in the woods? (no commas)

10 The vases (,)which were not packed properly(,) were damaged in the post. (optional commas)

Exercise 11
1 preparation
2 disapproval
3 increasingly
4 reduction
5 hygienic
6 minimise
7 bacterial
8 attractive
9 convenience
10 irresistible

Unit 8

Exercise 1
2 will not be sent any money until next month
3 The children are being looked after by Aunt Dorothy
4 Have you been informed about the change of plan
5 My wallet was stolen by my brother
6 Milk and flour must be added to the eggs
7 you know who *The Sting* was written by
8 wasn't given any encouragement by his father
9 suddenly realised that we had been tricked
10 The suspect was being interviewed by Inspector Jarvis at 10 o'clock this morning

Exercise 2
1 was beaten in the final
2 were not married
3 was born in
4 warned us
5 was the mobile phone invented
6 is owned by
7 are building a new hospital
8 was I not told
9 were made of
10 are employed by IBM

Exercise 3
1 C	6 C	11 A
2 D	7 D	12 D
3 A	8 C	13 C
4 C	9 D	14 B
5 B	10 B	15 D

Exercise 4
2 'll know
3 are going to redecorate
4 's going to crash
5 is going to take off
6 will own
7 'm going to keep
8 'll help
9 is going to die
10 will steal

Exercise 5
1 at
2 same
3 of
4 has
5 are
6 been
7 become
8 to
9 There
10 start
11 off
12 both
13 whom
14 from
15 the

Exercise 6
2 So do we
3 So should Gordon
4 Neither/Nor can you
5 So do I
6 Neither/Nor could we
7 So might Simon
8 Neither/Nor do I
9 So will she
10 So am I

Exercise 7
1 I did not need
2 would be surprised
3 would never speak
4 they were treated well
5 she had some friends
6 would see her more often
7 the car were/was cheaper
8 were good
9 she knew you better
10 would be able

Exercise 8
2 shines
3 moved
4 would grow
5 sinks
6 would you promise
7 wouldn't buy
8 will say
9 wasn't/weren't
10 would taste

Exercise 9
1 ✓	6 no	11 for
2 the	7 then	12 ✓
3 from	8 a	13 that
4 do	9 ✓	14 ✓
5 ✓	10 to	15 so

Unit 9

Exercise 1
1 vigorous
2 harmful
3 obsession
4 addiction
5 pleasurable
6 energetic
7 increasingly
8 nervous
9 membership
10 willing

Exercise 2
2 have been studying
3 haven't seen
4 have you been doing, have been playing
5 Has Tim finished, hasn't started, has been watching
6 have been trying, have you been, have been talking
7 haven't written, have been meaning, haven't had
8 Have you been crying, have been chopping
9 Have you read, haven't had
10 have been looking forward, haven't eaten

Exercise 3
2 have had
3 for years
4 Have you been eating
5 have you known
6 phone calls
7 has he sold
8 has fixed
9 since they left college
10 have been telling

Exercise 4
1 the	6 to	11 ✓
2 for	7 be	12 will
3 ✓	8 there	13 so
4 up	9 ✓	14 a
5 ✓	10 it	15 yet

Exercise 5
1 regrets taking on
2 only I hadn't lent
3 wish we hadn't missed
4 regret not going
5 only I hadn't bought

6 you wish you had said
7 regrets not working harder
8 only I had saved some
9 he regret selling
10 wish we hadn't brought

Exercise 6

1 A	**6** B	**11** C
2 D	**7** C	**12** D
3 B	**8** B	**13** B
4 D	**9** A	**14** D
5 A	**10** D	**15** C

Exercise 7

2 would you have done, hadn't been
3 would have died, had arrived
4 had put, would have shrunk
5 would have bought, had known
6 would you have got, hadn't given
7 would have slept, hadn't drunk
8 had scored, would have won
9 would have enjoyed, hadn't talked
10 wouldn't have remembered, hadn't said

Exercise 8

1 would have let you
2 hadn't gone
3 would have helped
4 had given him some encouragement
5 would have told you

Exercise 9

1 h	**4** f	**7** a
2 i	**5** g	**8** e
3 d	**6** c	**9** b

Unit 10

Exercise 1

1 for
2 ✓
3 that
4 off
5 ✓
6 up
7 being
8 ✓
9 them
10 ✓
11 be
12 rest
13 of
14 no
15 ✓

Exercise 2

2 needn't cook
3 mustn't open
4 needn't wash
5 must remember
6 must pay
7 mustn't use

8 needn't bring
9 must sign
10 needn't make

Exercise 3

2 should/ought to go
3 should/ought to see
4 shouldn't criticise
5 shouldn't let
6 should/ought to drink

Exercise 4

1 you have to
2 may leave the room
3 must stop
4 must not eat
5 shouldn't buy this house
6 can't understand
7 needn't take part
8 have to/must go to school
9 you may not go
10 really ought to be

Exercise 5

1 B	**6** C	**11** D
2 B	**7** A	**12** B
3 A	**8** D	**13** C
4 D	**9** B	**14** A
5 C	**10** A	**15** B

Exercise 6

2 allow
3 made
4 let
5 Allow
6 make
7 allowed
8 made
9 allow
10 let

Exercise 7

1 to
2 which
3 made
4 in
5 of
6 to
7 been
8 was
9 the
10 such
11 by
12 there
13 between
14 up
15 after

Exercise 8

2 wishes he hadn't lost his keys
3 wish the baby wouldn't/didn't cry all night
4 wishes she could drive
5 wish you a safe journey
6 wish I couldn't smell the pig farm next door

7 wish I hadn't bought an expensive car
8 wishes he didn't have to go to hospital
9 wish I was/were good at maths
10 wish you wouldn't (always) leave the garage door open

Exercise 9

1 wishes she could speak
2 wish you would do
3 wish I were
4 you have a pleasant
5 wish I wasn't
6 he hadn't given her
7 wishes he could afford
8 wish I lived on
9 wishes she had bargained
10 wish you all

Unit 11

Exercise 1

1 ✓
2 a
3 than
4 and
5 so
6 up
7 ✓
8 with
9 of
10 ✓
11 are
12 be
13 ✓
14 that
15 no

Exercise 2

2 told him (that) Lucy didn't want to see him that night
3 said (that) I was working for Harry that week
4 told us (that) we had to report to the office before we left
5 said (that) I hadn't known about the meeting the previous week
6 said (that) Mark hadn't spoken to his brother for two years
7 said (that) by the time we (had) got there all the food had gone
8 told me (that) he would phone me if he heard any news
9 told him (that) he could stay with her the following day, if he wanted
10 said (that) he had met Julie about seven years before/previously

Exercise 3

2 'You will have to ask permission'
3 'You can't go out tonight'
4 'I have been waiting for hours'
5 'I saw her once last week'
6 'I'm not going to work today'
7 'Mary will kill you if she finds out'

8 'It started to snow when I got up this morning'
9 'I left school years ago'
10 'I won't be able to help you until tomorrow'

Exercise 4

2 told him to stand up straight
3 asked me when I was going to buy a new car
4 asked Terry to help her with the baby
5 asked me if I was aware of the risks involved in the operation
6 asked her why she had painted her bedroom walls black
7 told him not to touch the electric fire
8 asked her where my yellow jumper was
9 asked me if I had heard what Jack had done the night before
10 asked her if she would be seeing Jeremy that afternoon

Exercise 5

1 A		**6** C		**11** D	
2 B		**7** A		**12** C	
3 D		**8** C		**13** A	
4 D		**9** B		**14** C	
5 C		**10** B		**15** B	

Exercise 6

2 offered to give her a lift home
3 admitted crashing into the garage door
4 refused to lend him a thousand pounds
5 promised to write to his mother every day
6 invited them to his party
7 suggested going to bed early that night
8 denied telling anyone about it
9 reminded Simon to go to the bank
10 warned him not to eat those mushrooms or he would be sick

Exercise 7

1 he had moved into
2 did not cheat
3 me whether I had met
4 for not recognising her
5 asked Thomas where he was
6 him not to try
7 Ted if he would
8 forget to bring your camera
9 him to be careful
10 you like to come/go

Exercise 8

1 is said (that)
2 is not believed to be
3 considered by anyone to be
4 is supposed to be
5 reported to have been injured
6 is said to be
7 is thought (that) the burglar
8 is understood to be
9 is not considered to be
10 know (that) this man is

Exercise 9

1 introduction
2 successful
3 ensure
4 starvation
5 survival
6 obtainable/obtained
7 frequently
8 profitable
9 explanation
10 cruelty

Exercise 10

1 had
2 place
3 at
4 what
5 into
6 with
7 WILL
8 did
9 out
10 later
11 when
12 by
13 was
14 it
15 in

Unit 12

Exercise 1

1 had
2 would
3 to
4 than
5 back
6 with
7 put
8 fact
9 for
10 on
11 still
12 a
13 of
14 except
15 so

Exercise 2

2 doesn't she
3 didn't we
4 could he
5 have you
6 shall we
7 will you
8 can we
9 will you
10 weren't they
11 won't you
12 did he
13 won't I
14 is it
15 shouldn't we

Exercise 3

1 A		**6** B		**11** B	
2 A		**7** C		**12** B	
3 C		**8** C		**13** D	
4 D		**9** A		**14** A	
5 B		**10** D		**15** D	

Exercise 4

2 would be
3 was going to
4 would be
5 was about to/was going to
6 were on the point of
7 was going to
8 was to/was going to
9 was going to
10 were to/were going to, would be

Exercise 5

1 not
2 ✓
3 there
4 that
5 ✓
6 it
7 they
8 out
9 ✓
10 quite
11 such
12 a
13 ✓
14 time
15 to

Exercise 6

2 I don't
3 Do be quiet (children)
4 does want to play in the team
5 likes sailing, but Fred doesn't
6 does work hard at school
7 does look like his father
8 did go to university
9 eat meat, but John does
10 Do phone me as soon as you arrive

Exercise 7

1 were wiped out by/in the Ice Age
2 before he took to his new surroundings
3 will sort out any further problems
4 digital watches has dropped off/is dropping off
5 caught up with the kidnappers as they were trying to leave the country
6 we could get by if it wasn't for mother's part-time job
7 broke out on the fifth floor of the building
8 finally turned up at midnight

Unit 13 Test 1

Exercise 1
1 B
2 A
3 B
4 D
5 D
6 C
7 B
8 A
9 B
10 C
11 D
12 C
13 A
14 C
15 B

Exercise 2
16 one
17 such
18 like
19 each
20 few
21 that
22 could
23 in
24 of
25 his
26 into
27 later
28 back
29 on
30 out

Exercise 3
31 must have/get my hair
32 isn't/is not warm enough
33 wish I had accepted
34 she was being followed
35 in case you get
36 might have had
37 look after the dog
38 apologised for not writing
39 you mind holding this
40 allow me to visit

Exercise 4
41 over
42 for
43 it
44 ✓
45 have
46 with
47 ✓
48 to
49 ✓
50 they
51 of
52 the
53 ✓
54 up
55 a

Exercise 5
56 boredom
57 occasionally
58 behaviour
59 psychologists
60 peaceful
61 abusive
62 enrage
63 overtaking
64 invasion
65 personal

Unit 13 Test 2

Exercise 1
1 B
2 A
3 D
4 D
5 C
6 C
7 A
8 B
9 B
10 D
11 B
12 D
13 A
14 B
15 C

Exercise 2
16 and
17 to
18 with
19 which/that
20 little
21 would
22 in
23 takes
24 between
25 from
26 have
27 on
28 the
29 as
30 afterwards/after

Exercise 3
31 whose car this
32 on the point of falling
33 regrets not saving/having saved
34 must/have to be picked up
35 what she had done
36 if you had not/hadn't encouraged
37 had such a quiet voice
38 did not/didn't use to go
39 must not run
40 can't/cannot have taken

Exercise 4
41 be
42 ✓
43 that
44 the
45 he
46 about
47 ✓
48 of
49 ✓
50 being
51 ✓
52 to
53 ✓
54 it
55 you

Exercise 5
56 introduction
57 various
58 cultural
59 players
60 willing
61 effectively
62 anyway/anyhow
63 Furthermore
64 undeserving
65 famous